# sexual subjects

# sexual subjects

....................................................

## lesbians, gender, and psychoanalysis

**adria e. schwartz,** Ph.D.

ROUTLEDGE

*New York and London*

IKL

S

Published in 1998 by
Routledge
29 West 35th Street
New York, NY   10001

Published in Great Britain by
Routledge
11 New Fetter Lane
London EC4P   4EE

Copyright © 1998 by Routledge
Printed in the United States of America on acid-free paper.
Book design by Charles B. Hames

**Library of Congress Cataloging-in-Publication Data**
Schwartz, Adria E., 1946–
    Sexual subjects : lesbians, gender, and psychoanalysis / Adria E.
Schwartz.
      p.   cm.
    Includes bibliographical references (p.      ) and index.
    ISBN 0–415–91092–7 (hb.) — ISBN 0–415–91093–5 (pbk.)
    1. Lesbians—Identity.   2. Lesbianism—Psychological aspects.
3. Gender identity.   4. Feminist theory.   5. Women and
psychoanalysis.    I. Title.
HQ75.5.S39   1998
155.3'33—dc21                                97–21490
                                                CIP

*to my son Alex . . . for being Alex*

This book is dedicated to the women and men with whom I have worked in psychoanalysis and psychotherapy, and to my students and supervisees, who have taught me so much. It is through their collective generosity in allowing me to share in their experiences, and their courage in attempting to create new vistas, that this book became first a possibility and then a reality.

Finally, to my family of friends whose constant support and encouragement enabled me to persevere through dark moments, a very special *thank you.*

# contents

# preface

In the early 1980s, I sent a letter of inquiry to a contemporary psycho-analytic journal proposing an article on what I perceived to be the developing rapprochement between feminism and psychoanalysis. I received, as part of a rather harsh indication of negative interest, the following admonishment: "Feministic psychology has nothing to do with psychoanalysis." That was, of course, not quite true, as feminism had very much to do with early psychoanalysis, and very much to do with psychoanalysis and lesbians.

Today, feminism does inform psychoanalysis, not as a political plat-form, but as a tool in understanding gendering (Flax, 1993) and rela-tions of power within traditional gender hierarchies. (Benjamin, 1988; Foucault, 1980).

The psychosexual development of women became the subject of great debates within the psychoanalysis of the 1920s (Fleigel, 1986). Was femininity/heterosexuality a secondary development for women, as Freud (1925) would have it, or primary, as the psychoanalytic revi-sionists were to suggest (Horney, 1926; Jones, 1927, Klein, 1928; Riviere, 1929)?

Women were difficult to treat; perhaps not more so than men, but in a manner that remained elusive and frustrating. Feminist readings of Freud's early case of Dora (Moi, 1981) highlight the young patient's objections to being treated as a sex object, handed off between males at their convenience. Freud (1905), however, in his preternatural way, signals his own misreadings (countertransference) of the manifestations of Dora's desire in the postscript to the case: "I failed to discover in time and to inform the patient that her homosexual (gynaecophilac) love for Frau K. was the strongest unconscious current in her mental life" (p.143).

Both Freud (1920) and Jones (1927) refer to feminism in the rare instances in which they wrote about female homosexuality. But it was either *en passant*, as in Freud's case ("She was in fact a feminist")[1] or alluded to as evidence of a rather pesky pathology, as in Jones's (1927) paper on female development, where he is discussing one of two groups of homosexual women: "The familiar type of women who ceaselessly complain of the unfairness of women's lot and their unjust ill-treatment by men" (p. 467).

Today we recognize the foundational feminist premise that gender has served as a basic cognitive organizer in the culture (Kohlberg, 1966), and that gendering has played an integral part in the making of the individual subject (Flax, 1993). Yet there has been a longstanding resistance to that gendering and to the late nineteenth-early twentieth-century conflation of gender and sexuality.

Resistance to identity, (Rose, 1986) as it constrains sexual practice and gender performance, has been a significant feature of lesbian existence, as has resistance to compulsory heterosexuality (Rich, 1981). Much of *Sexual Subjects* is about that resistance, as it takes shape in the questioning of the construction of certain categories: woman, feminine, lesbian, homo/hetero/bi-sexual, mother.

Butler (1990a, 1993a) has made serious *Gender Trouble*, and its reverberations can be heard throughout this book. The subversion of the presumed mimetic relationship between sex and gender, a constructed body upon which is inscribed a socially constructed and performative gender, is reflected in the use of the collapsed term *sex/gender* throughout the text. The use of this term might seem at odds with another theme of the book: that serious misunderstandings about "female homosexuality" have been propagated by the conflation of sex and gender—a woman who desires another woman, must be a man, or like a man, or wants to be a man (Magee & Miller, 1992; O'Connor & Ryan, 1993). But that conflation is itself a function of the heterosexually based opposition of identity and desire. Wanting *to be* and wanting *to have* are continually counterpoised, both within psychoanalysis and the broader culture of which it is a part, in the hegemonic heterosexual construction of desire.

There is a tension inherent in writing about lesbians that pervades *Sexual Subjects*. There is the acknowledgment of the ongoing struggle of lesbians to affirm their subjectivities and their sexual/romantic practice within a psychoanalytic and surrounding culture in which they have been largely invisible. And then there is the strain of the recognition that the category *lesbian* is a modern creation, born of a certain discourse, founded within a certain historio/cultural location (Foucault 1978, 1980). The poststructuralist/postmodern critique of categories call the very necessity of the existence of lesbians into question. (Butler, 1990, 1993a; Dimen, 1991; Goldner, 1991; O'Connor, 1995; D. Schwartz, 1995a). *The Lesbian Postmodern* (Doan, 1994) both is and is not an oxymoron, as bodies and desires are reconfigured and metanarratives deconstructed.

Identity and resistance, agency and subjectivity circle round and round this category that is lesbian. For Wittig (1982), a lesbian is not a woman for she has not a woman's place in the gender hierarchy; for Butler (1990) the very category of woman is suspect. Should the concept of identity be abrogated altogether or seen as balanced by multiplicity (Benjamin, 1996)? Again there is the tension of what is usually referred to as identity, a coherence of self-organizations and -representations, and the internal discontinuities and diversities of self-states and desires. *Sexual Subjects* reflects my position, in agreement with Mitchell (1991) and Aron (1995), that we need both a notion of identity, which may or may not be gendered, stable and continuous over time, and a postmodern notion of multiple subjectivities (Flax, 1996) that can be fragmented and discontinuous as well.

Both modern and postmodern conceptions of gender and sexuality are reflected in the ensuing essays. Categories of sexual practice and gendering, as well as the determinative nature of physical bodies, are deconstructed on the one side; and specific issues that are problematic but nonetheless meaningful to self-identified lesbians—such as butch/femme roles, the privileging of genital sex, and "lesbian bed death" are examined within a larger context of lesbian eroticism.

Similarly, the deconstruction of the concept of motherhood, based as it is on a foundation of anatomy and desire, allows for the question: Is motherhood a gendered relation? The deconstruction of gendered motherhood allows us to envisage a new parenting subject that would be less unitary and more conditional, a conception of mothering that transcends gender—a shift from mothers to mothering ones. Moreover, the reconstruction of motherhood developed here implies the reconstruction of families as well. Mothering no longer rests within the confines of a heterosexual matrix.

In a similar vein, *generativity redux* addresses the conflations of femininity with motherhood and motherhood with generativity. These equations have acted as a bar to both creative and procreative generativity for lesbians. Within this essay, I speak to a variety of issues that impact on lesbians and generativity, including internalized homophobia as it retards creative agency; procreative issues; and a process I refer to as a de-identification with mother as female, which may also impede generative extension. The essay speaks to generative issues within lesbian families, as well.

The final chapter, "coming out /being heard," deals with the ways in which *coming out* may facilitate the unveiling of true self in the Winnicottian sense (Winnicott, 1960), but it may also serve to masquerade a more disavowed subjectivity. (Riviere, 1929).

The evocative debate resounding in the current psychoanalytic literature about the status of *the self* and its relation to postmodern conceptions of multiple subjectivities (Mitchell, 1991; Aron, 1995; Flax, 1996;
Harris, 1996) is not fully reflected here. In the text, I refer to more
authentic feeling self-states, and truer self-experiences, as modifications
that incorporate the spirit of Winnicott with our newer understanding
of the liminally discontinuous character of what used to be referred to
as *the self*. The emphasis in the essay, however, is on the foreclosure of
authenticity and the ways in which feeling unreal—a lack of agentic
subjectivity—can become encoded within the closeting of sexual desire.

A final word on the clinical material.

Clinical anecdotes are interspersed throughout the book. They are
not offered as detailed "case process," nor have I included then as "evidence" to support the positing of new scientific/truth-based theory.
Rather, the clinical anecdotes are put forth as corroborative illustrations
of certain narrative tropes that have arisen in my analytic and supervisory work over the years. My hope is that they might serve to enliven
the text, and to remind us that the subject is us.

**note**
1. As quoted in Harris, (1991), p 198.

# resistance

It is true that at Arras and Beaurevoir I was admonished to adopt feminine clothes; I refused, and still refuse. As for other avocations of women, there are plenty of other women to perform them.
—JEANNE D'ARC, in West, *Saint Joan of Arc*

coming out of silence to scream
to stand strong and proud
coming out of my gut
daring all
i will not be swept away
kept locked away in preconscious
i will come again
—CONSTANCE FAYE, *"Come Again"*

Within psychoanalytic discourse, lesbians have been most striking in their invisibility. In eschewing the traditional feminine position as objects of phallic desire, (Freud, 1925; de Beauvoir, 1952) and/or appropriating the phallus as it signifies subjective desire (Butler, 1993a), lesbians stand outside the laws of patriarchy and compulsory sexuality. In that space, they have rarely been represented as other than damaged or renegade (Harris, 1991).

Within the larger domain of western culture, sex/gender "refuseniks" seem to have disappeared into an abyss of historical detritus. It has been one the aims of feminist, gay, and lesbian historiography to reconstruct their histories within the context of that resistance (Daly, 1978; Katz, 1976; Duberman, Vicinus, & Chauncey, 1989).

An historical framework grounds our way of understanding the multiple meanings of lesbian sexuality to include the genderpolitical as well as the psychosexual. Within the spectrum of women resisters, there is a refusal of phallic primacy that has to do not solely with desire, but also with issues of agency, subjectivity, and their worldly manifestations in the form of power over spheres of influence and legitimacy as bestowed by dominant cultural institutions.

There have long been women resisters, identified through their refusal to adhere to or incorporate the traditional genderlinked binaries of subject/object, active/passive, male and female, once reified in psychoanalytic theory (Dimen 1991).

Working-class and peasant women of the seventeenth and eighteenth centuries wore men's clothing, "passing"as men, in order to gain greater freedom, earn more money, or do things that women couldn't, such as enter military service (Vicinus, 1993). Other women resisted sexual prescriptions by flagrantly indulging their erotic desires, paying little heed to the societal norms of the day (Taylor, 1991). The women might be of the nobility (Marie Antoinette), intellectuals (George Sand), courtesans of the nobility (Liane de Pougy), or women of the demi-monde, such as the love interest of Freud's (1920) young patient in his "Case of Female Homosexuality," who so aggrieved the patient's family by the implied seduction of their daughter.

The category *lesbian*, itself a term of indeterminate parameters (Golden, 1987; Burch, 1993; D'Ercole, 1996), can be subsumed within a larger, more loosely constituted category of resisters. During the height of lesbian feminist separatism in this country, lesbians were defined largely by that resistance.[1]

> A lesbian is the rage of all women condensed to the point of explosion. She is the woman who, often beginning at an extremely early age, acts in accordance with her inner compulsion to be a more complete and freer human being than her society—perhaps then but certainly later—cares to allow her. . . . She may not be fully conscious of the political implications of what for her began as personal necessity, but on some level she has not been able to accept the limitations and oppression laid on her by the most basic role of her society—the female role. (Radicalesbians, 1973, p. 240)

Adrienne Rich (1981), poet and feminist, suggests in her now classic essay, "Compulsory Heterosexuality," that the historical existence of lesbians, and the continuing attribution of meaning to that existence, signifies both the breaking of a taboo and the rejection of a compulsory way of life.

By compulsory way of life, Rich is referring, of course, to heterosexuality. Rather than viewing heterosexuality as the normative endpoint of psychosexual development, Rich emphasizes the inexorable pressures of economic, religious, cultural—and one might add psychological— institutions to be heterosexual. Lesbian existence then, in and of itself, is an act of resistance to those forces.

Considering lesbian existence as resistance to compulsory heterosexuality helps to shift our perspective from the medicalized continuum of normality/pathology where it has traveled for so long within psychoanalytic thought, to one that locates the category within a sociocultural and tempero/historical frame.[2] This is not to say that the category lesbian, as it refers to a history, a set of relationships, a set of sexual behaviors, fantasies, internal representations, or performative acts of resistance, has a universal signifier. It does not. Moreover, the spirit in which I discuss resistance carries within it the seeds of de(con)struction for any identity that fixes a parameter of sex/gender in place.

## resisters

In considering historical figures of resistance within the context of sexuality and gender, it might seem strange, at first, to see a reference to Joan of Arc. As a woman who has been appropriated by some as a virgin martyr, she is not a person who would come to mind while scanning the usual repertoire of sex/gender radicals. Yet, of late, Joan has been praised by some feminists as a successful refugee from the entrapments of gender and, more specifically, has been studied as a transvestite (Garber, 1992).

Joan of Arc (1412–1431) has been hailed as a visionary, admired as a military leader, condemned as a witch. She had her first vision at the age of twelve or thirteen; it was a vision that told her to drive the English out of France and install the Dauphin, later known as Charles VII, on the throne.

Joan struggled with these visions, at first telling no one. Finally, at the age of sixteen, at the alleged behest of St. Margaret and St. Catherine, she sought and gained the support of the Dauphin in her quest. In doing so, she disguised her sex, and dressed as a man. In 1429, sitting astride a white horse in a full suit of armor, she led 10,000 men in the successful defeat of England at the siege of Orleans.

Joan finds her place among the sex/gender radicals because she fought to be a "knight in shining armor" rather than await his coming. An oversimplification of a very complex woman living in a complex era, it's true. Yet in that aspect of her many incarnations, she presents an interesting icon through which to understand the notion of resistance, not only to compulsory heterosexuality (she refused to marry the man of her families choosing; it is assumed that Joan was a virgin) but the foreclosure of agency to women in her era. Garber (1992) notes, that among the final charges that led to her death by fire, were that she was immodest, and hence unwomanly, and that she carried with her weapons of defense. Joan of Arc, with the apparent blessings of God and her sister saints, refused to be the woman that fifteenth–century France prescribed. Hers were crimes of gender transgression read as heresy.

Christina, Queen of Sweden (1626–1689), was a scholar and accomplished linguist. She was also a skilled equestrian and hunter. Christina ascended to the throne early in her teens, and at the age of eighteen had herself crowned "king," a title she deemed worthy of greater esteem. Although she dressed in men's clothes and seemed to envy male privilege, Christina was uncomfortable with its accouterments and the egregious inequities of power and wealth that she felt had accrued to the royal house. She sought to redistribute wealth by giving away money and lands—much to the distress of the aristocracy, under whose prodding she ultimately abdicated ten years later.

Queen Christina had as her constant companion and "bedfellow" her lady-in-waiting Ebba Belle Sparta. She was open about her female lover, "one whose mind was as beautiful as her body" (Taylor, 1971, p. 23). They spent much time traveling in Europe, where Christina continued to resist the constraints of her society by consorting with Jews— another group of marginal members of her culture, at best.

Resisting the constraints of the gender binary (Flax, 1993), Christina wanted to be king instead of queen; she persisted in being the subject of desire rather than its object and demanded recognition of that position by "openly flaunting her liason." Yet she eschewed the more traditional trappings of phallic power and resisted its hierarchy, as it was manifest in gender or class or religion.

Natalie Barney, "queen" of the Paris salons in the 1920s, looked to the Greek poet Sappho as her muse. A woman of independent means, Natalie created the Academie des Femmes, a Parisian salon devoted to the support and cultivation of women artists and writers. Through her salons at the infamous 20 Rue Jacob, she introduced members of the Academie to publishers, gallery owners, and each other. Of equal importance, she provided an audience for their work (Benstock, 1986). Natalie hoped to nurture a society that would be defined by its female denizens—a society free of what she conceived of as the male imperatives of marriage and reproduction. In her own way, Natalie's life and work was a living embodiment of resistance to what Rich articulated some fifty years later as compulsory heterosexuality (Wickes, 1977; Benstock, 1986).

Natalie rejected the masculine cross-dressing of some of her lesbian contemporaries. Her argument was with what she perceived to be the dominant patriarchy, not with being a woman or the variegated signifiers of femininity. She personally was attracted to women of the demimonde, an elite group of prostitutes, courted by noblemen and princes who lived in a world constructed both as product of the patriarchy and as rebellion against it.

A lover and seductress, she had many affairs—appalling local society by her so-called flamboyance, which to Natalie meant, "to live openly, without hiding anything" (Benstock, 1986, p. 272). Natalie Barney embraced her desire and was desiring.

Across the sea, far in every way from Barney's Paris/Lesbos, the Harlem Renaissance was underway, and women, women loving women, were major figures in it.[3] Gladys Bentley was of particular interest both as a figure in the Harlem Renaissance and as a resister.

Philadelphia-born musician and cabaret-style blues singer, Gladys ran away from home to Harlem at the age of sixteen. Sometimes performing as herself, sometimes cross-dressed and appearing as Bobbie Minton, Bentley performed at the Clam House and the Ubangi Club. "Unlike her lesbian contemporaries in the entertainment field, Bentley proudly acknowledged her lesbian sexuality. She packed her 250 lb. frame into a tuxedo, flirted with women in her audience, and dedicated songs to her lesbian lover" (E. Garber, 1988, p. 31). Bentley, resisting racial taboos as well as gender and sexual interdictions, lived openly with her white lesbian lover, eventually marrying her in a highly publicized wedding ceremony.[4]

In sum, St. Joan became France's knight in shining armor but was killed because of her gender transgressions. She refused the retiring modesty of womanhood and the garb that acted as its signifier. Queen/King Christina, Natalie Barney, Gladys Bentley—each in her own way rebelled against the asymmetric sex/gender binary and compulsory heterosexuality of the dominant culture. Gladys Bentley resisted not only gender privilege but also the privileges of race and class, as well.

## resistance and psychoanalysis

But, one might ask, what does any of this have to do with psychoanalysis? In 1984, in an article advocating a rapprochement between the then—adversarial forces of psychoanalysis and feminism, I wrote:

> The psychoanalytic inquiry assumes the primacy of gender ascription and infantile sexuality in the developing object relations of the

infant and significant other, and uses the psychoanalytic dyad to
revivify those experiences. . . . [F]eminism informs psychoanalysis
so that the reconstructive journey traces development within a context of political/cultural and historical reality, and delineates the
ways in which that reality is transmitted, transferred, interiorized
and recreated within the individual and/or collective system under
study. (A. Schwartz, 1984, p. 11).

Implicit there, but not yet fully delineated, was a social constructivist
approach to sexuality and gender, informed by attention to the contri-
bution of culture to what was then more often thought of as "sex-roles,"
a concept that linked an essentialist perspective with a sociological one
(Sherif, 1982). What seems a truism in some quarters now was more
radical then, as mainstream psychoanalysis largely turned a deaf ear to
the voices of both the feminist theorists in this country and the post-
structuralists abroad (Lacan, 1977; Derrida, 1978; Foucault, 1978).

Now, informed by the postmodern critique, we question not only
essentialist notions of the sex/gender binary but also the very privileging of gender as foundational to personal psychology or sexuality
(Schoenberg, 1995; D. Schwartz, 1995a; Flax, 1996).

Institutional psychoanalysis, more so than its individual theoreticians
or practitioners, has a long history of resistance to challengers of the
asymmetric sex/gender binary and the privileging of heterosexuality
(Lewes, 1988; O'Connor & Ryan, 1993).

It was not until the 1990s—almost two decades after the American
Psychiatric Association removed homosexuality from the diagnostic
manual and decried active discrimination against homosexuals—that
the American Psychoanalytic Association's executive council finally
endorsed their position statement (Flaks, 1992). Even then, seventy
years after Ernest Jones rejected a gay applicant for psychoanalytic
training because he believed that the applicant's sexual orientation was
pathological and could not be corrected by analysis, the American
Psychoanalytic Association was loathe to condemn the exclusion of

homosexuals from training institutes. In 1992 the American Psychoanalytic Association reluctantly adopted a nondiscriminatory policy to ensure that gay men and lesbians could rise through the ranks of their training. The policy linked the homophobia of the psychoanalytic/psychiatric establishment to sexism, stating that its roots "lie in the hatred of what I perceived and labeled as feminine in men" (Isay, 1989, p. 128). And although lesbians are nominally included in the more current protests against gay exclusion within the psychoanalytic establishment, lesbians have remained largely invisible in the discourse.

But—times are changing.[5]


## psychoanalysis as feminist subject

With the advent of *Psychoanalytic Dialogues* in 1991, and the concomitant burgeoning of the relational approach to psychoanalysis, the poststructural/postmodern critique has found its way out of the halls of the academy and into the consulting room.[6] What once appeared as the "bedrock" of the psychoanalytic understanding of gender and "mature" (hetero/genital) sexuality is no longer foundational. The bedrock is not so much crumbling as, upon closer inspection, made of sand.

The relational theorists have emphasized that gender/sexuality develops in and through relationships with others (Mitchell, 1988, 1991). Discarding the constraints of a one-person psychology and viewing gender from a relational perspective, theorists have understood that cultural fantasies and practices in the realm of gender/sexuality help to mold the the interpersonal and systemic matrices out of which persons grow (Goldner, 1991). In concert with the postmodern critique of Enlightenment assumptions, new questions arise as to the privileging of a unified psychic world and the reification of a coherent, consistent, discrete gender/sexual identity (Butler, 1990b; Goldner, 1991; Harris; 1991).

Given a new freedom of language in which to rethink fundamental tenets, the discourse within psychoanalytic gender/sex thinking has begun to shift.

In *Disorienting Sexuality* (1995), Domenici and Lesser have assembled a unique collection of papers that, in sum, question the hegemony of heterosexuality in the construction of gender/sexuality within the culture and its representatives in psychoanalysis.[7] Informed by postmodern critiques, Foucault (1978, 1980), social constructionism, and feminist and queer theory, the papers are by no means monolithic in their viewpoint. However they converge in their largely consensual view that lesbian, gay and heterosexual identities are historio/cultural productions rather than endogenous psychic structures.

Coming from another direction—that is in reaction to the poststructuralist assault on the determinative self, Mahoney and Yugvesson (1992) utilize a relational analysis of subjectivity to understand the phenomenon of resistance. Relying on the work of Winnicott (1971) and Stern (1985), they envisage the child as an active constructor of meaning and not as solely determined by the power/knowledge constraints of hegemonic discourse. Power relations produce conformity. They can also evoke resistance. Mahoney and Yugvesson (1992) argue for a theory of agency in which dependence is a condition of independence and inequality is a condition of resistance:

> It is in this potential space between self and other, first experienced by the infant with the transitional object, that play, creativity, and agency (understood as the invention of new meanings) are made possible. This understanding of playfulness as the ground for resistance helps explain how the strategies of "parodic proliferation" of gendered meanings described in Butler's (1990) work are possible (p. 62).

This relational subjective approach acknowledges the tension between the performative aspects of gender and the gendering of internal representations that are the result of our intersubjective and object relations. Moreover, it allows for both elements of identification and resistance.

Acts of resistance require a subjectivity that is capable of choosing marginalization and dislocation. De Lauretis (1987) envisages such a subject as one that possesses the potential to stand both within and outside the sex/gender discourse. For De Lauretis, such a subject is labeled feminist, but in a strange way, much of the forward movement of relational psychoanalysis aspires to be such a feminist subject.

## notes

1. This occurred in the United States roughly in the 1970s through the mid- to late-1980s.

2. For additional references on the pathologizing of homosexuality in psychoanalytic thought, see Mitchell (1981); Flaks (1992); O'Connor and Ryan (1993); Magee and Miller (1992); Blechner (1993); Domenici (1995).

3. Gladys Bentley, Ma Rainey, Bessie Smith, Ethel Waters, and Alberta Hunter all had sexual affairs with women.

4. According to Eric Garber's (Spring 1988) article in Outlook magazine "Gladys Bentley . . . The Bull Dagger Who Sang the Blues," Bentley seemed unable to withstand the psychological and economic pressures of McCarthyism. In August of 1952, she wrote an article in *Ebony* magazine entitled "I Am A Woman Again" in which she claimed hormone treatments got her out of a "life of hell" and into a life as a happily married heterosexual. This marriage, to a cook 16 years her junior, lasted 5 years, after which she apparently gave up on her sexuality and devoted herself to the Temple of Salvation in Christ. She died in 1960.

5. For example, in January 1997 in New York City, the Society for the Study of Social Trauma and Psychoanalysis presented a symposium entitled Homophobia on the Couch: Psychoanalytic Perspectives on Homophobia in Clinical Practice, in which homosexuality was no longer viewed as a phenomenon of clinical interest but rather as a rigid, pathological defense against recognizing same-sex erotic interests within the psyche.

The Spring 1997 Meeting of the Division on Psychoanalysis of the American Psychological Association sponsored symposiums on Race, Sex and Power; Psychoanalysis as a Regulatory Practice; the Interaction of Culture and Psychoanalytic Concepts; and Developing Desires: Female Sexualities in Cultural Contexts.

6. A psychoanalytic journal of relational perspectives, published by Analytic Press.

7. This volume was the result of a fairly unique conference sponsored by the New York University postdoctoral program in psychotherapy and psychoanalysis on December 4, 1993, where openly gay- and lesbian-identified psychoanalysts—as well as analysts who did not declare a sexual preference—presented papers.

# a lesbian is . . . a lesbian is not

Some psychoanalytic theories tend to construe identification and desire as two mutually exclusive relations to love objects that have been lost through prohibition and/or separation. Any intense emotional attachment thus divides into either wanting to have someone or wanting to be that someone, but never both at once. It is important to consider that identification and desire can coexist, and that their formulation in terms of mutually exclusive oppositions serve a heterosexual matrix.

—BUTLER, "Imitation and Gender
Insubordination"

The literature of homosexuality usually fails to distinguish clearly enough between the questions of the choice of object on the one hand, and of the sexual characteristics and sexual attitude of the subject on the other, as though the answer to the former necessarily involved the answer to the latter.

—FREUD, "Psychogenesis of Case
of Female Homosexuality"

To refuse to be a woman, however, does not mean that one has to become a man.

—WITTIG, "One Is Not Born a Woman"

How is it that some women so profoundly resist their place in the scheme of things—the "natural" place of their sex and gender (Dimen, 1995)? Psychoanalysis returns again and again to Freud's Dora (1905a), who resisted what she perceived to be her fate as an *objet de refuse* at the hands of the adults around her. Dora resisted not the "talking cure" itself but the relentlessness of Freud's oedipal interpretations and his determination to have her psyche fit his theories, rather than the other way around. And as Freud was later to realize, Dora resisted the dismissive denigration of her love for Frau K, the "homosexual current" in her psychic life.[1]

Freud wrestles with other resisters. In his "Case of Female Homosexuality" (1920), there are actually two. The first is the object of analytic inquiry; the other is the agent provocateur, with whom Freud has no contact. The "patient" is nameless, a voiceless young woman (she never speaks for herself), somewhat "masculine" in her intellect (that is, apparently sharp and incisive), and a feminist, according to Freud, because she protests at the inequities of gender privilege. She is sent for treatment to Freud by her parents, as she proclaimed herself ready to throw herself upon the rail tracks for the love of the wanton and seductive woman she loved.

This lady, another resister—a "demi-mondaine" as Freud referred to her—transcended the law of the common bourgeoisie by having affairs with both men and women. She flaunted her sexual prowess and the pleasure she obtained through it. Not content to be confined or defined solely as an object of men's desire, she appropriated their phallic subjectivity by expressing her sexual desires as well.

Resistance strikes at the core of a gendering of sex and desire as it is prescribed by the culture and its various institutional representatives. Resistance to the gendering of bodies often brings one to the brink of madness, it seems, as our transsexual, transgendered, hermaphroditic self-representations threaten to destabilize our very cognitive organizations.

## mrs. g

Robert Stoller (1973), a respected psychoanalytic expert on sex and gender, presents extensive transcripts of verbatim sessions with Mrs. G, a married, "bisexual" mother of two who was convinced that she had a penis. In an early session, Stoller tried to prove to his patient that it is logically impossible for her to have a penis, because she is a woman. Mrs. G. responds:

> Why worry about this one little thing? It's not hurting anybody. . . . And it's not hurting me. It's not a delusion. It's inside me. This is something I've always known, and I've always felt, and it's there, and it's real, and it's mine; and you can't take it away from me, and neither can anybody else, so you might as well kiss my ass. (p.15)

After some questions about whether Mrs. G. has had daydreams about her penis, she senses that this is a trap designed to place her penis in the realm of fantasy. Mrs. G. becomes angry:

I have this. I have it and I use it and I love it and I want it and I intend to keep it and there's nothing you can do about it. It's mine. It makes me what I am. (p. 15)

When Mrs. G asks Stoller why he continues to bother her, he replies: "I want you to be normal." (p. 17)

SHE ASKS AGAIN: "Why does it hurt? It doesn't hurt anybody." (p. 17)
STOLLER REPLIES: "It prevents you from being a woman."
MRS. G. ANSWERS: "No it doesn't. I can screw a man just the same as any other woman." (p. 17)

Mrs. G's penis is her protection. It keeps her safe and strong, not vulnerable like other heterosexual woman. It is a somatic concretization of the phallus that she wants and rightly assumes that men (psychiatrists included) don't want her to have. In a way, Mrs. G's "mental illness" foreshadows Judith Butler's (1993b) work, and more specifically her essay, *"The Lesbian Phallus and the Morphological Imaginary."* However, Mrs. G is not about philosophy or gender theory but rather about her desperate attempts to find alternative ways of being a women.

The appendix of Stoller's book lists among the gender disturbances of masculine women: the butch homosexual woman (diesel dyke); the unrealized transsexual; the transsexual woman; women with penises; conflating lifestyle and libidinal prefences with issues of body dysmorphia and more fundamental reality testing.

Today psychoanalysis hears and is responding to a poststructuralist/postmodern protest that is barking at the heels of the dominant culture. The *trans*vestite . . . *trans*sexual . . . *trans*gendered ask that we valorize phenomenological experience of sex/gender and deconstruct their performative aspects. The inviolate biological truth of the gendered material body is inviolate no longer.

And with the flowering of identities within a polymorphously perverse, queer universe, the notion of a sexual identity becomes increasingly evanescent. It is indeed an interesting condition when Jan Clausen (1990), a lesbian-identified writer, comes out as a pregnant dyke who is sleeping with a man. She claims to be a man-loving lesbian in a relationship with someone whom she identifies as a "male sperm bearing lesbian."

It would seem that the sex/gender system as we have known it is being dismantled, and many, even within the halls of psychoanalysis, are beginning to question whether there remains any meaningful use at all for the construct of sexual identity (Schoenberg, 1995).

## a lesbian is . . .

In one of the few extant reviews of the psychoanalytic literature on female homosexuality, Magee and Miller (1992) point out that the assumption that "a woman who loves a woman must be a man, or be like a man, or must want to be a man" underlies many of the formulations of lesbianism. Psychoanalytic thinkers have long suggested that lesbians are male identified, thinking they are or wish to be male (O'Connor & Ryan 1993, p. 67).[2]

Freud's (1905b, 1908) theory of psychosexual development required all girls to surmount the hurdle of their primary masculine/clitoral sexuality, defining the libido as masculine in nature, and the clitoris as functioning as a penis in childhood. True femininity, a feminine sexuality that is embedded within a heterosexual reproductive matrix, became a developmental achievement. Failures along this developmental path left a girl at risk for a masculine/(homo) sexuality (Freud, 1920).

Jones (1927) and Horney (1924, 1926), among other revisionists, saw femininity as primary rather than a developmental achievement, and could envision a female sexuality that was independent of masculine origins. However female (hetero) sexuality was conceived, be it essentially or as a psychic construction, the occurrence of unmitigated phallic jealousy or a precipitous retreat from the oedipal, resulted in the girl forsaking her father as a libidinal object and taking him as an object of identification instead. And it was this identification that rendered her at risk for homosexuality.

In his paper on the development of early female sexuality, Jones (1927) categorized as homosexual women who wish for "recognition" of their masculinity from men, and women who claim to be to be the equals of men or, in Riviere's words, "to be men themselves." (Riviere 1929, p. 305).

Jones maintained that there are two different groups of homosexual women. Members of the first group manifest little or no overt interest in men. Their libidos center on women, and he postulates that they use women as a way of covertly enjoying their own femininity. These women have allegedly given up the male (paternal) as a libidinal object, instead making him the identifying object. Women are wooed as a means of preserving a femininity that has been renounced, partly as a defense against incestuous wishes.

The second group of homosexual women retain their interest in men but set their hearts on being accepted by them as equals. To this group Jones ascribes the feminists, "the familiar type of women who cease-lessly complain of the unfairness of women's lot and their unjust ill-treatment by men" (Jones, 1927, p. 467). The aim in this group is to obtain recognition of their identification—that is, to be treated as "one of the guys."

According to Jones, a child confronting the oedipal taboo is forced to either *have* the object or *be* it.[3] Female homosexuality evolves flight from the oedipal via male identification. For women, the search for recognition or validation by men for one's equality is interpreted as a sign of male identification, which in turn becomes a signifier for female homosexuality. Jones's formulation is presented as representative of a longstanding psychoanalytic paradigm in which sexual orientation is conflated with gender identity, each fixed in their unipolar modalities, and of a paradigm in which femininity has been collapsed within het-erosexuality.

Fifty years later, the substratum of the theory prevails. According to McDougall (1980), for instance, homosexual girls give up their fathers as objects of love and desire and identify with him instead. In this way, "the daughter acquires a somewhat fictitious *sexual identity*; however, the unconscious identification with the father aides her in achieving a stronger sense of *subjective identity*. She uses this identification to achieve a certain detachment from the maternal imago in its more dangerous and forbidding aspects" (p. 87). McDougall herself calls this explanation oversimplified, and in a more current reading one can see that what she is alluding to more accurately is identificatory love, whereby the girl attempts to identify with the "father of separation, the representative of the outside world" (Benjamin, 1988, p. 108).

Benjamin (1995) makes clear that identificatory love is a pre-oedipal identification for a toddler girl, rather than an oedipal appropriation of the penis in order to woo the mother. It is an attempt to embody separateness from mother and escape the helplessness and dependency that she may represent. McDougall makes this error because she, like Jones (1927), insists that one must either *want/desire* the other or *be* the other. Normative heterosexuality admits no other alternatives.

What seems to unify many psychoanalytic theories of homosexuality is that they reify "a gendered split between desire and identification, between having and being, such that identification with one gender appears to require desire of the other, and desire correspondingly seems to imply opposite-gender identification" (O'Connor & Ryan, 1993, p. 55). The construction of identification and desire as two mutually exclusive relations supports a normative heterosexuality (Butler, 1991, 1993a). Moreover, the theory presumes a unitary subject who makes a unified, discrete, and coherent gendered identification through incorporation or internalization.

There is within traditional modernist psychoanalytic theory the conflation of gender and sexuality, what Freud characterized as "the choice of object on the one hand, and of the sexual characteristics and sexual attitude of the subject on the other" (Freud, 1920, p. 170). More recently, psychoanalysts informed by feminism and object relations theory have begun to reconceptualize the development of gendered identifications. There is a growing realization that the conception of gender identity as fixed, uniform and coherent is a conception that either pathologizes or denies multifaceted gendered aspects of internalized object relations as they are manifest in dreams, fantasy, and more direct phenomenological reports (A. Schwartz, 1989; Dimen, 1991; Goldner, 1991; Benjamin, 1995).

Benjamin (1988) clearly states that object choice does not define gender identity: "the core-sense of belonging to one sex or the other is not compromised by cross-sex identifications and behaviors. The wish to be and do what the other sex does is not pathological, nor necessarily a denial of one's own identity. The choice of love object, heterosexual or homosexual, is not the determining aspect of gender identity, an idea that psychoanalytic theory does not always admit" (p. 113).

To cite another example, Bassin's (1996) amended schema of gender development allows for a body-ego experience that is both differentiated and overinclusive. As the child moves toward a more consistent gender identity based on an identification with same-sexed parent, she simultaneously moves away from the restrictions of gender based on an early, overinclusive, body-ego experience with the psychically nongenitaled parent and forms identification with the parent of the "opposite" sex.[4]

But even as psychoanalysis twists and bends to accommodate to a more flexible concept of gendered identity, one that is more consonant with the actualities of psychic life, outside of the psychoanalytic domain there continues to be active resistance to compulsory membership in one or the other of the gender categories—or to the categories themselves. Popular culture in the 1980s and '90s has been fascinated with the downing of gender barriers: on stage, *M Butterfly*; on film, *The Crying Game*; in text, Garber's (1992) *Vested Interests*, to name a few. In academia, the debates in feminist circles and in gender and queer studies have been fast and furious as the politics of identity vie with the general deconstruction of coherent categories in the postmodern arena.

Monique Wittig, a renowned lesbian theorist of Marxist persuasion, claims that lesbians are resisters, but not women. Wittig suggests that the category lesbian does not have to do with women loving other woman, but rather denotes the refusal to assume a place in a heterosexual gender system that defines the necessary relations between the sexes. If one does not occupy a place in that heterosexual gender system, then one is perforce not a woman.

In her now near-classic essay, "One Is Not Born a Woman," Wittig (1981) places lesbians totally outside of the gender categories. Using the material feminism of Christine Delphy and Simone de Beavoir as her referents, she refutes essentialist claims to the biological categories of sex, male or female: "The category 'woman' as well as the category 'man' are political and economic categories not eternal ones" (p. 15). According to Wittig, lesbians need to extricate themselves from the "natural" parts of being female that are imposed upon them.

The essence of her argument is that *woman* is not a natural biological category but a class, a political and economic ideological category that serves a certain societal function, and one that is rejected by lesbians. She quotes de Beauvoir, in *The Second Sex*:

> One is not born, but becomes a woman. No biological, psychological or economic fate determines the figure that the human female presents in society: it is civilization as a whole that produces this creature, intermediate between male and eunuch, which is described as feminine. (de Beauvoir, 1952, p. 249)

For Wittig (1982), sex itself is a category produced in the interests of the heterosexual contract. The lesbian, in her subjectivity, has rejected the woman's place in that gender hierarchy. Being a woman, according to Wittig, means occupying a certain place of subordination and servitude in the system. "The category lesbian thus does not have to do with women loving women, but rather a position that challenges the necessary relation between gender and sexuality created by and essential to heterosexuality" (Roof, 1991, p. 248).

Wittig points out that, by resisting the oppression that she sees as intrinsic to the category woman, lesbians become subject to the label of being "not real" women and/or being accused of wanting to be men. Attempts by women to destabilize phallic privilege are thus demeaned: "To refuse to be a woman, however, does not mean that one has to become a man" (Wittig, 1981, p. 12). Lesbians refuse either position in the gender hierarchy as undesirable. "Thus a lesbian *has* to be something else, a not-woman, a not-man, a product of society, not a product of nature, for there is not nature in society." (p. 13).

Wittig maintains that it is only the lesbian subject who has transcended the confines of the gender binary. She universally dismisses the concept of the ontological difference between the sexes and calls for a "a new personal and subjective definition for all human kind" (Wittig, 1981, p. 20). A true individual subjectivity will be possible only when the categories of sex no longer exist.

## on the cusp of the postmodern

Wittig stands on the cusp of the postmodern. She struggles to escape what she perceives as the discourse of "The Straight Mind" (1980) as it manifests itself in universal totalizing interpretations of history, culture, language, social reality, and psychoanalysis.

The *postmodern condition* as described by Lyotard (1984), is marked by a crisis in knowledge and belief, which is expressed as an "incredulity towards metanarratives" and "the obsolescence of the metanarrative apparatus of legitimation" (p. xxiv). According to Lyotard, metanarratives operate through a system of inclusion and exclusion, forcing a kind of homogeneity and the privileging of truth (Storey 1993). The postmodern critique calls for a dismantling of these universal totalizing narratives and replacing them with an increased plurality and diversity of voices and perspectives.

The lack of certainty about what is true and universal in the natural and social sciences has allowed for the shifting, erosion, and multiplication of traditional categories and constructs. In the same year that Lyotard published his *Postmodern Condition*, feminist/anthropologist Gayle Rubin launched her challenge to what she has called our sex-value system:

> Modern Western societies appraise sex acts according to a hierarchical system of sexual value. Marital, reproductive heterosexuals are alone at the top of the erotic pyramid. Clamoring below are unmarried non-monogamous heterosexuals in couples, followed by most other heterosexuals. Solitary sex floats ambiguously. Stable, long-term lesbian and gay male couples are verging on respectability, but bar dykes and promiscuous gay men are hovering just above the groups at the very bottom of the pyramid. (Rubin, 1993, p. 12)

Sexuality as a socially constructed discourse that included notions of homosexuality, and hence lesbians, did not really exist until the late nineteenth century. During that time, sexology emerged as a bona fide academic discipline in which homosexuality fell under medical purview and became a sign of nervous degeneracy (Faderman, 1993, Domenici, 1995).[5] Of course, there had been longstanding religious taboos specifying who might couple and with whom, but, as Rubin (1984) points out, these strictures related primarily to forms of kinship, designating proper unions to sustain particular social organizations. When medicine and psychiatry became culturally ascendant, the concern shifted from unfit unions to unfit forms of desire (Rubin, 1993, p. 12). Sexual terms like *homo*sexuality, *hetero*sexuality, or *bi*sexuality were not always with us. They are products of a certain evolving discourse and can only be seen properly when viewed through the lens of their historical and social contexts.

Rubin credits Foucault (1978) and his enormously influential *The History of Sexuality* with her understanding of discourse formation, and his work is indeed fundamental to the more current dialogues within psychoanalysis. Simply stated, Foucault sees power operating through discourse, and the parameters of a particular discourse are always rooted in power. Foucault rejects what he calls the "repressive hypothesis" of power, in which the state is viewed as repressive and censoring. Rather, for Foucault, cultural institutions function as *producers* of knowledge and truth, the definers of domains of reality (Foucault, 1979, p. 27).

Foucault argues that the different discourses on sexuality are not *about* sexuality, they actually *constitute* sexuality. This is not to say that sexuality does not exist. The ways in which we understand sexual relations, however—our "knowledge" of sexuality—are discursive (Storey, 1993).

Following the path forged by Foucault, Butler (1990a, 1991, 1993a, 1995) presents a comprehensive deconstruction of the sex/gender system as a function of a hegemonic heterosexual discourse, where sex has been construed as biologically determined and gender is socially constructed. She disrupts the relationship between sex and gender, introduces the concept of gender as performance, and critiques what she interprets as the valorization of gender identity within psychoanalysis.

Butler suggests that there is no necessity for gender to retain a mimetic relationship to sex, given that the former is presumed to be culturally constructed and the latter biological. Thus, man and masculine might just as easily signify a female body as a male one; and woman and feminine might just as easily signify a male body as a female one. Culture has always recognized this, in fact, and we have always had our "masculine" women and "feminine" men with differing roles and differing levels of approbation or proscription, depending on the culture. Butler (1990a) extends her analysis even further, however, and calls into question the distinction between a supposedly biologically given sex and a culturally constructed gender:

> Can we refer to a "given" sex or a "given" gender without first inquiring into how sex and/or gender is given, through what means? And

what is "sex" anyway? Is it natural, anatomical, chromosomal, or hormonal? . . . Does sex have a history? Does each sex have a different history, or histories? Is there a history of how the duality of sex was established, a genealogy that might expose the binary options as a variable construction? . . . If the immutable character of sex is contested, perhaps this construct called "sex" is as culturally constructed as gender; indeed, perhaps it was already gender, with the consequence that the distinction between sex and gender turns out to be no distinction at all. (pp. 6–7)

## gender as performance

Concomitantly, then, Butler challenges the very notion of an intrapsychically grounded gender identity. Far from a developmental achievement based on a series of identifications and internalizations, as the predominant gender theorists within psychoanalysis would maintain, (Freud, 1925, 1931; Stoller, 1968; Tyson, 1982; Fast, 1984; Benjamin, 1995), Butler (1990a) sees gender as largely performative. Given that behavioral acts, gestures, and expressions of desire in our culture are gender coded, Butler claims that it is the interactive sum of these gendered acts and gestures, that produce the effect of internal substance. However, this effect is produced on the surface of the body. The gendered body is performative in the sense that the essence of the identity that it purports to express becomes a "*fabrication* . . . manufactured and sustained through corporeal signs and other discursive means" (p. 336; emphasis in original).

A "butch" woman, a man in drag, calls into question the very nature of the binary gender system and destabilizes phallic privilege. Traits attributed to masculinity do not require being a male, just as behavior attributed to femininity does not require a female body. For Butler (1990a, 1993a), the gendered body has no ontological status apart from these performative acts that constitute its reality: "And if that reality is fabricated as an interior essence, that very interiority is a function of a decidedly public and social discourse, the public regulation of fantasy through the surface politics of the body" (1990b, p. 336). Butler boldly claims that the illusion of a core gender is created and sustained in order to regulate sexuality, that is, insure the reproduction of heterosexuality.

Butler seeks to resist the force of gender fixities. She disputes the existence of an interior gender identity as it appears to emerge within classical psychoanalysis: a gender identity that is reified as a developmental achievement with a certain "normative" path; a coherent discrete identity that appears to foreclose gender complexities and disruptions as they occur. She cautions us to beware "the myth of interior origins, understood either as naturalized or culturally fixed" (Butler 1990b; p. 339).

Partly, it is a question of paradigms (Kuhn, 1962). In the past two decades, paradigms have seemed to float amid a sea of theory and practice. Psychoanalysis has shifted in its conception of itself from a science (Freud, 1895) to be conceptualized as a theory of psychosexual development (Freud, 1940), a clinical method of inquiry bent on deconstructing the patient's experience (Levenson, 1992), a seeker first of historical and then narrative truth (Spence, 1982), a social-constructivist enterprise that enriches the analysand's subjectivity and knowledge of self (Mitchell, 1993; Hoffman, 1991)—to name a few of the operative paradigms.

Butler critiques the more classical psychoanalytic paradigm that valorizes the notion of identity, particularly gender identity as a developmental achievement, while she questions the very validity of the concept itself. Here, she is in keeping with the postmodern critique, which calls into question even the most apparently basic categories such as woman, in that they privilege gender above the intersection of gender with race, class, ethnicity, age, sexuality, and other currents that may be more or less relevant given certain temporal and cultural locatedness (Flax, 1993, 1996).

Butler (1990b) accurately challenges the developmental narratives of psychoanalyses by asserting that whether one begins with Freud's primary bisexuality, or the primacy of object relations (Chodorow, 1978; Benjamin, 1988), the narratives construct a same-sexed identification (mother/daughter; father/son) and opposite-sexed desire, which in turn reproduce a normative heterosexuality:[6]

> The construction of coherence conceals the gender discontinuities that run rampant within heterosexual, bisexual, and gay and lesbian contexts in which gender does not seem to follow from sex, and desire or sexuality generally, does not seem to follow from gender; indeed, where none of these dimensions of significant corporeality 'express' or reflect one another. (Butler, 1996a, p. 336)

Clinicians might well argue, however, that the postmodern critique of unitary transtemporal notions of self and identity are sometimes in conflict with the phenomenology of self and identity experiences as they emerge in the consulting room, where there is often a pull on the part of the analysand toward an experiential sense of unity and cohesion. However, clinicians might then realize as well that a sense of cohesiveness of self does not necessarily require a *fixed* gender identity of always and totally female or male, or a *fixed* sexual identity of gay, straight, or bisexual. These fixities do not meet with the reality of human experience or desire, which are varied, changing, and evanescent within the nonlinear, nonrational, representational language of the unconscious.

Benjamin (1995) warns us that throwing out the concept of a unified identity doesn't mean throwing out a concept of identification as internal process. Butler (1995) herself, in clarification of her theory of gender as performative, recognizes the need for interiority in the discussion of gender. With this work, she more closely approaches newer psychoanalytic understandings of the interfluidity of heterosexual and homosexual identifications (D. Schwartz, 1995b).

## a lesbian is not . . .

A decade ago, when writing about the development of female gender-role identity, I differentiated the following constructs which were in concert with then-current gender theory: core gender identity, gender role identity, and object choice. *Core gender identity*, a term introduced by Stoller (1968) that refers to the fundamental knowledge that "I am a girl" solidifies somewhere before the end of the second year, and has since been more aptly understood by Benjamin (1995) as *nominal gender identity*. *Gendered role identity* was defined as an internalized gendered sense of self that is multiply determined by biological, cultural, and psychological factors, known as *gender role identity*; and *object choice*, the selection of an object of desire. At that time, I noted that "Gender role identity involves an internal self-evaluation of . . . femaleness and is thus continuous rather than discrete, mutable in a way that core gender is not" (A. Schwartz, 1986, p. 58).

Since that writing, and through the postmodern and deconstructionist influence, we have been expanding our notions of gender to be even more fluid, less unitary. To quote Harris (1991):

> The position that I am suggesting is one in which gender is neither reified nor simply liminal and evanescent. Rather in any one person's experience, gender may occupy both positions. . . . Furthermore, there may be multiple genders or embodied selves. For some individuals these gendered experiences may feel integrated, ego-syntonic. For others, the gender contradictions and alternatives seem dangerous and frightening and so are maintained as splits in the self, dissociated part-objects. . . . Gender, then, and the relation of gender to love object can be understood only by acts of interpretation. In that way the density of their unconscious and conscious elaborations are brought into the realm of language. (pp. 212–213)

Yet, people entering psychoanalysis or psychotherapy are sometimes troubled by a lack of coherence in their sense of gendered identity.

They seek some consonance between their gender as it is constructed by them and as it is perceived in the public eye. They sometimes find it difficult to tolerate the fractured, fragmented multiplicities of self, especially if they are internalized in negative form.

## not female like mother . . .

One particular identification that surfaces often but not exclusively among lesbians is the feeling that they are "not female like (their) mothers." Such an identification is ambivalently held and is not solely a proud label of resistance, as Wittig (1992) might presume. It is a double-edged sword, demonstrating not only resistance, a kind of refused identification (Butler 1995) but more painful, but also a renunciation of the maternal and those aspects of "femininity" that might otherwise hold a positive valence in relation to their body-ego.

Identities based on being not female like (their) mothers often coincide with negative body images, as their bodies are perceived to be out of synchrony with gender stereotypic icons. As gender is written upon the body, being not female like mother devolves into having bodies that must of necessity be of masculine caste and hence inadequate.

Here, I am primarily referring to a particular group of lesbians who share a similar constellation of early family experiences, out of which spring similar unconscious paths to gendered identifications. The women to whom I refer grew up in families where gender roles were fairly rigid and fixed and were perceived unconsciously as oppressive and noxious by mothers who responded, in most cases, by depression and withdrawal. Mothers were not viewed favorably as objects of desire and rarely appeared as agentic subjects. The men, on the other hand, seemed to embrace their instrumental roles as provider and liaison to the outside world and so continued to be perceived as effective and as occupying a privileged position. The daughter's ensuing de-identification with her mother played a part in developing an adult lesbian who felt disjunctive within herself and rejecting of those parts that are associated with being female like mother.

Clinically, the consequences of such de-identifications are often not problematic until an intimate relationship is sought. Then the denial of relational and specifically nurturing needs, the repressed anger, the defensive rigidity requisite for any renunciation, blocks the free give and take necessary for spontaneous human relatedness.

Developmentally, the period that extends from approximately fourteen to fifteen months into the second year is marked by—in addition to the development of language and the capacity for rudimentary representation—a growing recognition of both separateness from primary caretakers and the consequent vulnerability that ensues from the toddler's confrontation with the failure of her omnipotence in relation to herself and the world at large (Mahler, Pine, & Bergman, 1975; Stern, 1985). During this period, too, comes the emerging nominal gender identity (Benjamin, 1995), the knowledge that she belongs to that fundamental category known as "girl," which is accompanied by heightened awareness of the genitalia both in relation to gender difference and the potential for sensual pleasure.

According to Kaplan (1978);

> The girl discovers the sexual difference under the impetus of first discovering the pleasures of genital self-stimulation. The primarily exploratory and boundary seeking type of genital manipulation of the ten to twelve month old girl has by sixteen months been converted into a focused pleasure seeking activity. Now, with self/other awareness, the girl connects her frustrations as well as her delights with a person who might be contributing to them. As with the person-associated emotions of joy, anger and sadness, pleasure seeking genital arousal has the potential of becoming associated with other people. . . . The discovery of the pleasure possibilities of her own genitals at around fifteen or sixteen months impels the girl to become aware of the genitals of others and to ascribe meaning to the awareness. (p. 212–213)

Notice that for Kaplan, sexual difference is nearly synonymous with genital difference—a remnant of Freud's phallocentricity in that other embodied gender markers are rendered insignificant. However, what remains true is that, by the age of eighteen to nineteen months, the toddler is capable of making cognitive distinctions between genders and ascribing meaning to these distinctions.

Notice the timing here. During the same period that the toddler is dealing with the shame and frustrations of the failure of her omnipotence ("The world is not my oyster") and negotiating a new relationship of independence from her mother or other primary caretakers, she also confronts the anatomical differences between the sexes (privileged as those differences remain in this culture) and the social construction of gender. Quite a handful for the not-yet-two year old!

The danger of this period in terms of identity is that difficulties in negotiating this period will become linked to gender.[7] Successful negotiation of this period is vital for the development of object constancy, for a boundaried, positive, ongoing sense of self in relation to others, for the ability to tolerate ambivalence and the integration of sexual and aggressive feelings.

As Chodorow (1978) and Dinnerstein (1977) have so eloquently pointed out, women are (and, twenty years later, continue to be) the primary mothering ones in our society. Whether this actually occurs in a particular household is of course significant, but individual situations do not totally ameliorate the effects of a culture where women continue to be the primary caretakers (grandmothers, aunts, nannies, day-care workers, preschool teachers). This asymmetry in parenting does have a significant effect on the psychological development of both sexes and, of course, takes its toll on the parents as well.

During this period the toddler tends to blame both herself and the mothering ones for disappointments, the daily shames and humiliations, the letdowns and frustrations. She will alternately seek out and reject her caretakers as she struggles with yearnings for independence and mastery—yearnings that are as counterpoised as they can be with wishes to regress to an earlier, less complex state of relation (Mahler, Pine, & Bergman, 1975). A depressed, unavailable mother, a narcissistic mother who is able to relate to her daughter only as a self-object, will present stumbling blocks for the child through her empathic failures.

Thus, the possibility arises for the establishment of a destructive cycle where feelings of not-getting are confused with not-deserving (as female and/or angry female child) and aggressive wishes are confused with damaging effect (castration, as in permanent object status). When, in certain circumstances, this negative cycle is associated with gender, the groundwork is laid for the process of de-identification with mother as female.

The emergence of triangulation (the expansion of an essentially dyadic to triadic relational world) predates what has been the traditional "oedipal" period (Stoller, 1968; Abelin, 1971, 1980; Kleemann, 1976). Triangulation, in this context, connotes a developmental period marked by the incorporation of significant others into the object world of the child, the blossoming of genitality, the emergence of more clearly differentiated erotic object choices, and the establishing of more coherent gender role identities.

Traditionally, for the girl, the oedipal phase has referred to a turning or a shift in erotic object choice from the mother to the father, with accompanying feelings of rivalry and jealousy. However, as these shifts occur with greater and lesser frequency and intensity throughout the triangulation period, as the girl turns toward the father or significant others outside the mother-daughter dyad, one must inquire not only about shifts in object choice but also about the vicissitudes in identification and concomitant internal psychic representations integral to emerging gender role identity.[8]

Where this type of de-identification occurs, mothers, because of their own difficulties, appear to have epitomized the negative female stereotypes of passivity and general inadequacy in worldly matters. In their family constellations, the asymmetry of gender privilege was initially mystified by a quasi sado-masochistic dynamic, where men represented activity and effectance, strength and excitement, and women were weakness and constriction, paralleling and reinforcing cultural stereotypes.

Little girls as well as boys can identify with the family member who appears socially valued, competent, independent, and free from the risk of humiliation and contempt. Like her generic brother (Freud, 1931; Chodorow, 1978), this identification is based on being not like mother, an active dissociation from the female world.

During the period of triangulation, the young girl to whom I ascribe these conflictual identifications attempts to gain her father's respect and interest by proving that she is not female like mother. She can become the apple of daddy's eye—not by "accepting her femininity" (Freud, 1931; Fast, 1984) but by resisting and distancing herself from it.

Some disclaimers are in order here. This particular scenario, a composite that emerges from twenty years of analytic, therapeutic, and supervisory cases with women who are self-identified as lesbian, is in no way an endorsement of the frequent psychoanalytic split of desire and identification (Butler, 1995). This process of de-identification, of asserting oneself as not female like mother, is not a simple inversion of the allegedly normative oedipal progression leading to heterosexuality, also known as the "negative oedipal" (Roth, 1988). Nor is what is being described simply a manifestation of Benjamin's (1988) identificatory love, though it shares elements of each, as the young girl seeks to retain her subjectivity, which is perceived as being in opposition to the female gender role as embodied by her mother in the context of the world she sees around her.

This process of de-identification with mother as female involves the repression of nurturant needs, the precocious development of pseudo-independence, and a denial of relatedness. The narcissistic and depressed mothers of such children often collude, seeing the premature emergence of independence as a lessening of nurturant demands they feel unable or unwilling to meet. The de-identification is often accompanied by a project of saving or protecting Mother, accomplished by not-needing or not-wanting, by being strong, capable, and good. Moreover, the young girl is more easily able to retain mommy as a good object if she is successful in splitting off much of her rage at the empathic failures of the rapprochement period. In the service of the process of de-identification, and in the interests of the project of "saving mommy", some assume the role of caretaker, the idealized good parent silencing the more authentic voice of an angry crying child.

In positive mother-daughter relations—where the inequities of cultural male privilege are buffered by loving nurturant relations and a relational model of maternal agency and subjectivity, where there is a tolerance of ambivalent feelings and hence no overwhelming need to split off hostile feelings from loving ones, which would facilitate the reification of a bad mother and idealized father—positive female identifications will no doubt be internalized. There is no reason not to identify with a provider of good things, where mother and daughter are equally valued. Nor is there any need to abandon women as the primary love object(s), though much effort will be expended to persuade the girl that men should be the sole repository of her sexual desire.

Fathers and significant male others, in the positive affirmation of the girl's tentative sexual advances, may also help her to consolidate her sense of being both subject and object of desire. Moving out into the world, increasingly able to join and leave mother, the little girl has an "other" on whom to exercise her many creative skills and abilities. The quality of the mirroring of those abilities and skills, the reception or lack of it, their enhancement or denigration by the significant males and females around the child, will inevitably be linked to gender, subjectivity, and the apprehension of gender role.

Adolescence may be another crucial period in the formation of gender-role identities (Levy-Warren, 1996). Erikson (1950) termed this stage one of *identity* versus *role confusion*: "The integration now taking place in the form of ego identity is, as pointed out, more than the sum of the childhood identifications. It is the accrued experience of the ego's ability to integrate all identifications with the vicissitudes of the libido, with the aptitudes developed out of endowment, and with the opportunities offered in social roles" (p. 261). He points out that the adolescents must confront problems of *ideology* and *aristocracy*, which for Erikson means "the best people will come to rule and rule brings out the best in people" (p. 263). It is just this confrontation with ideology and aristocracy, better known in feminist circles as *patriarchy*, that is decisive for many young lesbians.

What is it, then, that the pubescent girl faces the dawn of her womanhood? Bodily changes are accompanied by heightened sexual desires, dreams of love and romance. Too often, however, she experiences heightened desire at more or less the same time as she encounters heightened sexual objectification by adolescent boys, forced once again, in a recapitulation of their earlier development, to "prove their manhood" by sexual conquest and renewed contempt for and denigration of women. With the expansion of social and educational spheres, the young lesbian is reacquainted with the overvaluation of the male world in sports, the media, and the corporate, academic, and military establishments.

It is during this time, too, that many girls are forced into more traditional roles of which they had been free during childhood. Mothers of lesbians who had been content to let their daughters "run wild," so to speak—to be tomboys or otherwise deviate from cultural norms—may become frightened and guilty during their daughters' adolescences. Within this period, mothers invariably feel the resurgence of their own psychosexual and role conflicts as their sexual and gender identities come into question through the feelings, attitudes, and behaviors of their daughters.

Adolescence too, is the time when fathers and/or other significant males recognize their daughters as sexual women, and it is a time when heretofore hidden or denied misogyny often comes to the surface. A paternal view of women as objects worthy of sexual desire or derision—his defenses against his own sexual interests in his daughter—can lead to a hypervaluing of the adolescent's sexuality so that it engulfs her definition by its presence or it absence. For young girls whose relationships with father in reality or fantasy have been based on collusion, a conspiracy of acceptance based on being not like her, not female like mother, for those lesbians, the fall from grace is devastating.

This adolescent lesbian (not all adolescent lesbians, or *the* adolescent lesbian) slowly and painful realizes in articulated or preconscious form that the asymmetry of gender privilege that she sees around her is reflected in her family as well. To be like him is to be the oppressor, to be like her is to be the victim. The earlier unconscious identification of not female like mother remains unchanged as she searches for a way out of this psychic limbo.

The assumption of a self-affirming lesbian identification seems to present one option, offering the possibility for reparation of early empathic failures and the expression of subjective sexuality. However, successful fulfillment of this possibility is often impeded by the early de-identification with mother as female, which engenders conflicts in expressing needs to lovers and the denigration of relational styles that have been equated with weakness and inadequacy, powerlessness and vulnerability.

In clinical work, it is necessary to address the gendered splitting (Dimen, 1991) as it is represented in the internal world. The working through of more primitive rage and despair at various empathic failures increases the ability to differentiate character from gender and gender from role, and facilitates a more textured understanding of sources of active resistance.

Understanding the father's position in the family constellation as dominant by virtue of both his role as carrier of male privilege and his individual dynamics enable the lesbian in analysis to differentiate assertion from sadistic aggression and otherwise to validate alternative forms of subjectivity that are not necessarily constitutive of gender.

### clinical anecdote

A lesbian in her mid-thirties who has struggled with gender issues, is painfully "not like other women" but is ambivalent about wanting to be. To her, being a woman is partly about "having to wait around to be fucked," yet she longs occasionally to be the object of her lover's desire and fears that she will never truly be because . . . she is not really a woman.

In the third year of analysis she brings in this dream, proudly announcing it as her first authentic lesbian dream. "A woman opens my vaginal lips with her fingers and adorns my clitoris."

She cites this as her first lesbian dream because in this dream she is the object of a woman's desire. "Men were not necessary to validate my femaleness." She continues, "Usually after a sexual dream I feel a violent wind going through me . . . but now things feel calm and safe. . . ." "It's not that I'm a man. I'm a different kind of woman. . . . I don't have to make myself a man to be different from her [the lover]. It makes me think of my mother. . . . Maybe this whole 'men' thing I created in order to be different than her. . . . If I'm a boy then I don't have to be skinny. I don't have to be like her . . . don't have to be sad . . . like she is. . . . My father was happier, sunny. . . ."

And about her lover, "We're different kinds of women . . . we have different ways of being female . . . different ways of being sexual. . . . this dick thing—the fantasy—it has no longevity. . . . It's not going to work."

## Notes

1. For additional commentaries on Dora, see Ramos (1980); Rose, (1978); and Moi (1981).

2. Psychoanaysis is changing. More current approaches to theories of gender and sexuality are reflected in Domenici & Lesser (1995); and Glassgold & Iasenza (1995).

3. Jones reformulates the castration threat as the threat of aphanisis, the annihilation of sexual pleasure.

4. Bassin's theory assumes heterosexual dual parenting and heterosexual orientation.

5. According to Faderman, the sexologists' creation of the category *lesbian* began in the 1870s. Intensely romantic frienships and "Boston marriages" that had flourished during the late nineteenth century were no longer condoned or socially acceptable, lest they be labeled "lesbians." For a fuller account of these relationships, see Faderman (1981).

6. Both Chodorow (1994) and Benjamin (1995) have more recently acknowledged the inadequacy of their respective narratives for understanding the development of heterosexuality, in the former, and homosexuality, in the latter instance.

7. For interesting, though controversial clinical research with boys in this period, see Coates (1990) and Coates, Friedman, & Wolfe (1991).

8. I am not aware of any sustained clinical work with adult children of lesbian couples, and so the question arises: Would this phenomenon of de-identificaion with mother as female occur in lesbian families, and if so under what conditions? What might processes of gendering be like for girls raised by two men?

# it's a queer universe . . . some notes erotic and otherwise*

> I have always wanted to be both man and woman,
> to incorporate the strongest and richest parts of
> my mother and father within/into me—to share
> valleys and mountains upon my body the way the
> earth does in hills and peaks.
>
> I would like to enter a woman the way any man
> can, and to be entered—to leave to be left—to be
> hot and hard and soft all at the same time in the
> cause of our loving. I would like to drive forward
> and at other times to rest or be driven.
>
> —AUDRE LORDE, *Zami: A New Spelling*
> *of My Name*

*A version of this article appeared in *Psychoanalysis and Psychotherapy*, *13*(2) (1996).

How do we understand Audre Lorde in the prologue to *Zami*, a "bio-mythographical" tale of her struggle as a West Indian girl growing up in New York City, finding her way as a black woman and a lesbian? She draws from the wellspring of her masculine and feminine identifications to enjoy a sexual subjectivity that is both active and receptive, that is penetrating, embracing, and desirous of being "driven."

According to McDougall (1986), "Homosexual desires in children of both sexes always have a double aim. One is the desire to possess, in the most concrete fashion, the parent of the same sex, and the second is the desire to be the opposite sex and to possess all the privileges and prerogatives with which the opposite-sex parent is felt to be endowed" (p. 219). Yet Lorde eschews that basic binary model, embedded as it is within a heterosexual matrix, by celebrating her womanhood.

> When I sit and play in the waters of my bath I love to feel the deep inside parts of me, sliding and folded and tender and deep. Other times I like to fantasize the core of it, my pearl, a protruding part of me, hard and sensitive and vulnerable in a different way. . . . Woman forever. (Lorde, 1982, p. 7)

We are unused to the clitoral imagery, and are apt to mistake it for phallic (Kulish, 1991). Lorde, however, reflects an internal bodily representation that holds a facet of lesbian eroticism, the essence of which is that it transcends what psychoanalytic theory has sought to label an infantile notion of undifferentiated bisexual completeness.

It has been difficult, however, for psychoanalytic theory to transcend a binary gendered world in order to don the lens necessary to recognize the underpinnings of the lesbian imaginary.

Fast (1984), in a critique of Freud's theory, presents a developmental model of gender-identity acquisition based on differentiation and the falling away of infantile notions of omnipotence, of limitless possibility. In her theory, Fast proposes an undifferentiated and overinclusive early matrix of gender representations where no attribute, physical or psychological, is excluded because it is gender inappropriate. Girls may imagine that they have a penis just as boys may wish or imagine that they have the procreative capacities that girls do. Having a penis, for a girl, does not negate her ability to nurture, nor alter her representations and identifications with mother and other things traditonally thought of as feminine. Fast takes issue with Freud's premise that girls, before acknowledging the anatomical distinction between the sexes, are "little men" and the clitoris an interior penile analogue (Freud, 1925). For Fast, however, the normative process of differentiation does involve coming to terms with the limits of one's biological sex (penis or reproductive organs; breasts seem to be absent) and the array of attributes culturally assigned to one gender or the other.

Thus, Fast would recognize Audre's pearl for the female organ that it is, but her expressed wish for bisexual completeness would be viewed by Fast as an indication of unresolved issues with childhood omnipotence. Fast finds residues of this early childhood's overinclusive and undifferentiated matrix of representations in bisexual myths, and primitive art (Fast, 1984, p. 17). Although Fast discusses the necessity of coming to terms with features of both biological sex and gender attributes, she deals with the former (i.e., male wishes to have babies, female phallic strivings) quite specifically, and only vaguely with the latter. The "girl must give up the possibility of having a penis and gender-inappropriate self representations" (p. 20). What those gender-inappropriate self-representations are, and what their relation to sexuality is, is never delineated by Fast. How one is to be a woman and how that womanliness is related to one's sexual aims are the heart of the matter for Zami and for the voiceless young woman in Freud's infamous "case of female homosexuality" (Freud, 1920; Harris, 1991).

Clinically and experientially, we know that bodily self-representations are vitally linked to sexuality and eroticism. Need they be linked to gender?

For Fast, identification with Mother's generativity seems to be the key both to female identification and to the shift in libidinal affections from mother to father. The wish for a baby from the father is not only an attempt at compensation for the girl's lack of a penis but also a manifestation of her identification with mother in her child-bearing capacity (Fast, 1984, p. 22). Thus, whereas Freud emphasized penis envy as the touchstone of female heterosexuality, Fast sees identification with biological reproductivity. But what of desire? Fast ignores, as Freud did not (1933), the "problematic" of the girl's continuing erotic tie to her mother. In Freud's model there is a constant pull toward the female homoerotic, but it is fraught with the baggage of "masculine identification." Fast rejects the phallocentricity of viewing the clitoris as a penile analogue, and with that rejection comes the rejection of the biological basis of Freud's theory of bisexuality for women: "In Freud's view the girl's central struggle is to overcome her masculinity; in the differentiation framework it is to overcome her narcissism" that is her sense of unlimited possibility (Fast, 1984, p. 32). Fast's notion of overinclusiveness conflates a multiplicity of wishes: to have male and female sex organs, to have the traits culturally associated with them, and to have access to a full array of sex objects (Aron, 1995).

It becomes the developmental task in this process of gender differentiation to work one's way out of the earlier state of infantile overinclusiveness and narcissistic omnipotence. And with this, according to Fast, comes an inevitable heterosexual path for desire. Fast's theory does not account for adult homosexual object choice in women.

Audre Lorde speaks to the tension between identity and desire. It is a tension that runs throughout (though in no way defines) lesbian eroticism and is not adequately explained either by Freud's phallocentrically based theory of innate bisexuality (which encompasses the gender-linked psychosexual attributes of activity and passivity) or by Fast's critique based on an essentialist model of gender differentiation (Freud, 1905b, 1937).

In her way, Lorde remains encapsulated in the "bi-ness"—bigendered, bisexuality—of our language. French feminists have attempted to write in or write about the necessity of formulating new language, which speaks to the specificity of the female body and female eroticism (Irigaray, 1985; Cixous, 1986). Wittig (1975) attempted, through fiction, to invent a language in which to speak exlusively about women's pleasure in women loving women. Although they speak from very different intellectual camps (Irigaray coming from an essentialist position, and Wittig from feminist/Marxist materialism), each struggles with the inadequacy of language to express female (Irigaray, 1985a) and specifically lesbian (Wittig, 1975) eroticism.

### the lesbian subject

The problem of language is inextricably tied to subjectivity. According to Case (1988–1989), the task of feminist theory in the 1980s was to deconstruct a subject position marked historically by masculinist function and simultaneously to construct a female subject position. Now, in the next decade, as postmodernism has gained sway in critical feminist and psychoanalytic circles, it is not the existence of a female subject that is at issue, but the possiblity of the female subject standing outside of her own locatedness so that she might be an agent of change. For De Lauretis (1987), it is this feminist subject "who is inside and outside of ideology of gender and conscious of being so, conscious of that pull, that division, that double vision" (p. 10) who offers the possibility of a transcendent subject.

Moving beyond De Lauretis, Case (1988–1989) suggests that it is the butch/femme couple who meets the requirements for the ideal, quintessential feminist subject—a radical claim, given the general sanction within the feminist community against butch/femme as a mark of continued heterosexist oppression within lesbian ranks.

Case refers to Riviere's paper (1929) to support her argument. In Riviere's now almost-classic case, (A. Schwartz, in press), a successful woman lecturer would follow each acclaimed public appearance by compulsive coquetry and by seeking approval from the older men in attendance. Riviere understood this to be an unconscious attempt at reassurance by this obviously bright and assertive woman, who had laid claim to the public arena, that she was in fact a woman (she had no penis); furthermore it served as a denial of her wishes to castrate the phallically privileged father figures in her midst.

According to Case, and it seems true, that within butch/femme scenarios, especially as they were constituted before the second wave of feminism and in their current retro-renaissance, women play on the phallic economy rather than to it. The lesbian roles are underscored as two optional functions for women in the phallocracy, whereas, as demonstrated by Riviere, the heterosexual woman's role collapses them into one compensatory charade (Case, 1989, p. 292). The agentic heterosexual woman adopts the masquerade of conventional nonagentic femininity so as to allay her own and others' fears lest she appropriate phallic privilege. With tongue in cheek, as it were, the butch in phallic regalia plays to the masquerading femme—each in disguise, each reveling in the not-knowing of what each other so clearly knows. As Case envisions the eroticism of this ideal lesbian subject, "the female body, the male gaze, and the structures of realism are only sex toys for the butch-femme couple" (Case, 1988, 1989, p. 297).

The theoretical debate continues as to whether butch/femme occupies a unique place outside the ideology of gender, as Case would maintain, or whether it represents a toxic residue of patriarchal oppression and sex roles with its tops and bottoms, its stone butches and feeling-carrying femmes. Rubin (1992) suggests that traditional stereotypes in the lesbian butch/femme community no longer hold—that it is not true that butches always desire femmes and must always "top" (that is, orchestrate the sexual encounters). There are femmes who maintain control, butches who seek out sexually dominant femmes or sexually aggressive butches; there are butch tops and butch bottoms, femme-femme partners and butch couples (Rubins, 1992, p. 471). The role play is intrinsic to the eroticism, it would seem, but, Rubin maintains that the issue is one of desire rather than of fixed gender identifications.

For Roof:

> Butch/Femme seems to be a resolution of the "inconceivability" of lesbian sexuality in a phallocentric system, recuperating that inconceivability by superimposing a male/female model on lesbian relations. . . .
>
> Butch/Femme, however, is internally self-contradictory from the beginning: inconceivability is nonetheless conceivable; a woman is nonetheless a man. What is important in the case of Butch/Femme is that the two processes—inconceivability and recuperation—and their internal contradictions coexist in a tension that never quite resolves itself, producing a systemic challenge to the necessary connection between gender and sexuality while appearing to reaffirm heterosexuality and forcing a consciousness to the artificiality and constructedness of gender positions. (1991, p. 245)

Hence, desire ripples off multiple identifications and object aims, forcing us to surrender notions of "femmunculus-like" monolithic internal objects, and to shift to notions of internalized object-relations, with the freedom to assume various identifications and seek after complex objects in a multigendered, internal arena.

In an interesting autobiographical essay, Jeanne Cordova (1992), a former nun and editor of one California's first lesbian feminist newspapers, traces her struggle to affirm her life as a "butch" within what she labels as the growing discrimination against this form of lesbian by feminist and lesbian feminist theory. The second wave of feminism broadened the acceptable boundaries of "real" womanhood with one exception: "I could be anything I wanted to be, except butch" (p. 290).

Cordova sees being butch as about resistance. Or, as she would put it, about being "ornery." As a five year old she was "ornery" and continued throughout her life to fight sex-role definitions and prescriptions. She defines butch/femme as the ornery spirit self that refuses definition, the core of a woman who transcends gender (Cordova, 1992, p. 291). Cordova rejects the blind identification of gender role with biological sex and seeks to create a multiplicity of genders that more accurately signal sexual desire and temperament:

> To me, a butch is a recombinant mixture of yin and yang energy. Like recombinant DNA, a butch is an elusive, ever-synthesizing energy field, a lesbian laser that knits the universes of male and female. Some have said feminist butch is an oxymoron. I say it's a paradox. A feminist butch is a dyke who has survived the Cuisinart blades of feminist rhetoric. To survive being butch you have to have been born with an ornery spirit. (p. 273)

When the illusion of being her father's "son" crumbled at puberty, Jeanne realized that as a daughter she was "superfluous in the scheme of family power" and that only men had what she wanted—power and money and women:

> I would eventually become a political activist, because my ornery
> spirit knew, long before my mind could explain, that our gay place in
> the world had been fundamentally misdefined. If men and women
> weren't divided and had it been gender were accepted as fluid, I
> wouldn't be perceived as deviating from a non existent norm. And nei-
> ther would the other one or two billion queers like me. (Cordova,
> 1992, p. 280)

Grahn (1984), another "butch" writing in the time of the feminist sex
wars, put it this way: "Our point was not to be men; our point was to be
butch and get away with it. We always kept something back: a high-
pitched voice, a slant of the head, or a limpness of hand gestures, something that was clearly labeled female. I believe our statement was 'Here
was another way of being a woman,' not 'Here is a woman trying to be
taken for a man'" (p. 31).[1]

Of these complementary gender performances, butch is obviously
the most transgressive in that it decenters phallic privilege; the femme
parodies but nonetheless operates within the realm of more traditional
womanhood. The femme doesn't challenge traditional gender role
ascriptions; her transgression is that she desires another woman.

Clearly, Case's position, that the butch/femme couple is the ideal
feminist/lesbian subject, is both radical and regressive. Butch/femme
does call into question the implicit connection of biology, gender, and
sexuality (Roof, 1991). However, proposing the butch/femme couple as
the ideal lesbian subject both obfuscates the wide range of actual lesbian
sexual practice and plays with, but ultimately does not transcend, the
confines of the heterosexually based gender binary.

## if the shoe fits . . .

This brief discussion of butch/femme (though far from a treatise on
representations of gender, nor their use within erotic scenarios)
brought to mind the countless clinical hours that have been spent in

work with lesbians on shoes, and the difficulty that many lesbians have in choosing, wearing, and feeling good about their fit.[2] Three instances come to mind:

One analysand, who painfully and ambivalently strained at the confines of traditional gender-role expectations, remembers that as a young girl she kept "losing her shoes," much to the dismay of her mother and her classmates awaiting her on the school bus. Interpreted as a passive-aggressive attempt to avoid school by her mother—the loss of her shoes, and most often one shoe—more accurately expressed both the analysand's sense of castrated helplessness in the face of a simultaneously intrusive and neglectful mother, and her rebellion at being forced into a type of femininity that did not fit. As an adolescent and young adult, she wanted only to wear "flip-flops"—rubber thong-like sandals that are unisexual and hence gender indistinguishable. Other shoes just weren't comfortable. Dreams were filled with images of casting off her shoes and running barefoot, free of filling both familial and gender expectations.

In another case, a lesbian who often complained of not feeling "like a real girl" claimed that she was only truly comfortable when wearing sneakers. The structure of her feet rebelled against the tightly fitting shoes common in women's fashion, she reported. She wouldn't be caught dead in high heels—designed to keep woman walking slowly, with an unsteady gait, appealing to but never competing with men. Her search to join a law firm (and implicitly what kind of work she would do) was partly determined by which office or larger work environment would allow her to wear her Reeboks. Terry maintained that she could never work anywhere where they required traditional women's dress; her feet just wouldn't fit "girls' shoes."

Yolinda, who into her third year of analysis talked about how she had never before purchased a pair of women's shoes, expressed her ambivalence and her wide-ranging sense of gender dysphoria most directly. A big-boned, somewhat large woman, she had, since adolescence, bought all of her shoes in the men's department. She had assumed that they would be more comfortable. Although this in itself never seemed problematic to her, she often complained about feeling ugly. On vacation with a new lover, and at a time when the subject of her womanhood was in the forefront in her analysis, she had "somehow decided" to enter the women's shoe department and found to her surprise that they had comfortable shoes to fit her as well. Modeling pumps, she took a new look at her legs. She liked their shape. They were woman's legs, she surmised with surprise and obvious pleasure. Then, Yolinda began to sob.

"I don't want to be a woman. If you're a woman you have to wait around 'til someone fucks you. You have to wait until someone desires you."

For differing reasons, none of these lesbians wanted to be in a woman's shoes. It was not a place of agency for them.

## polymorphous diversity

Literary anecdotal evidence and clinical data suggest that lesbian eroticism lives in a continuum of the polymorphously diverse that extends through more traditional variants of lesbian couplings, sado-masochistic practice, butch/femme enactments in and out of the bedroom, to the new Boston marriage where committed partners have little or no genital sex.[3] The use of the word continuum here makes obvious reference to, but should not be confused with, Adrienne Rich's original and somewhat idiosyncratic use of the phrase:

> "a range-through each woman's life and throughout history—of woman-identified experience, not simply the fact that a woman has had or consciously desired genital sexual experience with another woman. If we expand it to embrace many more forms of primary intensity between and among women, including the sharing of a rich inner life, the bonding against male tyranny, the giving and receiving of practical and political support . . . marriage resistance . . . we begin to grasp breadths of female history and psychology which have lain

> out of reach as a consequence of limited, mostly clinical, definitions of
> lesbianism. (Rich, 1981, p. 239)

Daring as this conception was in the very early 1980s, liberating women from the confines of heterosexually based genital sexuality while introducing the more agentic concept of resistance to a patriarchal limiting of the erotic for women, critics of the 1990s fear that such a definition "evacuates" lesbianism of any sexual content (Rubin, with Butler, 1994).

Roof's (1991) coinage of the phrase of *polymorphous diversity* more accurately describes the reality of lesbian sexuality. It not only differs among individuals—and individuals within race, culture, and class—but also is represented differently as history permits. Roof makes the point that lesbian sexuality exists as a coherent category only in contrast to heterosexuality and male homosexuality:

> Lesbian sexuality exists more at the interstices of multiple differences rather than necessarily constituting a core identity strong enough to completely fix an individual. Such an essential identity tends to come from outside—from phallocentric culture, for whom the category lesbian is sufficient. (p. 251)

From an intrapsychic perspective, one might say that lesbians retain women as primary objects of gratification, though not necessarily of identifcation. This does not exclude erotic connection to men, nor does it necessarily imply masculine identifications. Psychoanalytic theory has been based on the confluence of gender identification and object choice. Lesbian eroticism as theorized or practiced does not appear to be.

## resistance to identity

If one were to look at *Bar Girls*, a mainstream film distributed in the spring of 1995, what would one find? In it we are introduced to the characters in a women's bar in Los Angeles who are supposedly representative of the culture there—a potpourri of lesbians replete with pool tables, lesbians in "recovery," some brawling, and most seeking love.

There's Annie: a jock (athlete) who has been in a relationship with the same woman for eight years. They are celibate, however, allegedly because Annie's partner claims to be "straight." As the film progresses, Annie and her partner decide to have a more "open relationship" and the audience sees Annie with a variety of women as she seductively makes the rounds of the available sisters.

At the film's beginning, Victoria is also heterosexual, but she quickly becomes interested in women. She's very "femme" and picks out the "butch" from South Carolina who comes adorned with a black leather vest and Harley Davidson motorcycle. Throughout the film, they appear to be the most compatible and most committed.

Lorretta is desperate for declarations of love. Nonetheless, she is constantly being left by her partners. For her, love is sacred and she requires its declaration before she can have sex. There's Rachel, who is married to a man but who claims to be a lesbian. And JR, a "macho" police cadet who thrives on romantic conquest and the provocation of domestic disharmonies.

In true soap opera fashion, (seduction through the evocation of jealousy), Rachel flirts with Loretta and has sex with JR. The triangulation forces a heated separation between Rachel and Loretta, which is ultimately healed and understood as a defense against closeness. Lorretta also sleeps with JR in retaliation for what she experiences as Rachel's fear of closeness. Rachel and Loretta reconcile and become committed lovers themselves.

Men play no significant part in this movie.

*Bar Girls* seems to reflect the culture's splitting of love and sex. It is never quite clear whether the emphasis on seduction and conquest masks the need for affirmation and love, or whether the constant search for "love" is a way to make an aggressive sexuality legitimate in a culture where women are not to claim it for themselves nor desire it in another woman. But most clearly, *Bar Girls* could be seen as a movie about resistance, about the refusal to be locked into culturally constructed categories of gender role or sexual preference.

Jacqueline Rose (1986) has argued for recognition of the resistance to identity that lies at the heart of psychic life. She uses the concept to help define bisexuality as a sort of "anti-identity," an unconscious refusal to be limited to one object of desire or one form of loving. Daumer (1992), in an essay on bisexuality, speaks to the possible embodiment of that resistance in identity when she speaks about women choosing to re-create their sexuality with options that loosen them from the bonds of lesbian/straight, hetero/homo sexualities. "Because bisexuality occupies an ambiguous position between identities, it is able to shed light on the gaps and contradictions of all identity, on what we might call the differences within identity" (p. 98). For Daumer, bisexuality also allows us to problematize heterosexuality in ways that distinguish compulsory heterosexuality and efforts to resist heterosexualism within and without heterosexual relationships.

Identity, for Rose or Daumer, has little to do with gender and everything to do with the choice of sexual object and the identification with a group by means of sexual preference. In writing about lesbians, it is nearly impossible to escape the confluence of gender and desire.

Yet Daumer introduces an interesting perspective. For her, the construction of sexuality vouchsafes entrance into the "queer universe—in which the fluctuations and mutabilities of sexuality, the multitude of different, changing, and at times conflicting ways in which we experience our sexual, affectional, and erotic proclivities, fantasies, and practices can be articulated and acknowledged. In the queer universe, to be queer implies that not everybody is queer in the same way. It implies a willingness to enable others to articulate their own particular queerness" (Daumer, 1992, p. 100).

## bisexuality

It can be argued that part of Freud's radical genius lay in the manner in which he both theorized and clinically recognized the queer universe. Freud, following on the inspiration of his beloved nemesis Wilhelm Fliess, maintained a position of universal bisexuality, although the developmental foundation of that position changed as Freud's work matured from a biological to a psychic one—from a kind of infantile unisex containing both male and female aspects and erotically attracted to both, to a more mature lack of fixity in both identity and object choice (Garber, 1995).

Freud wrote:

> It is well known that at all periods, there have been, as there still are, people who can take as their sexual objects members of their own sex as well as of the opposite one, without the one trend interfering with the other. We call such people bisexuals, and we accept their existence without feeling much surprise about it. We have come to learn, however, that every human being is bisexual in this sense, and that his libido is distributed either in a manifest or a latent fashion, over objects of both sexes. (1937, p. 243–244)

Notice that Freud's views here are in the spirit of those of Helene Cixous (1986), the French feminist analyst who, some fifty years later, defined bisexuality as "the location within oneself of the presence of both sexes, that gives permission to multiple desires" (pp.84–85). Suleiman (1986) points out that Cixous's bisexuality is one of the "multiple subject who is not afraid to recognize in him or herself the presence of both sexes, not afraid to open him or herself up to the presence of the other, to the circulation of multiple drives and desires" (p. 16).

Ultimately, the difficulty in theorizing bisexual practice is that it assumes that the "object" in object choice has to have a one-to-one, mimetic relationship to the sex/gender binary. It might be said, though transgendered folks among others might disagree (Feinberg, 1993), that in everyday experience (which is our most common referent) one desires or has sex either with men, women, or both. Our conscious experiences seem to support reliance on the simple categories of homo/heterosexual (implying exclusivity in practice if not in fantasy) or of bisexual, implying an inclusiveness or lack of exclusivity.

But this simplistic conflation of gender and sexual orientation assumes a stable continuous, unigendered identity and a mimetic relationship of sex and gender that do not exist (Butler, 1990a; Harris, 1991; Zita, 1992). As our deconstructive efforts have amply demonstrated, internalized objects vary coterminously depending on what relation is being called upon for identification within the object love. Male/masculine identifications and female/feminine identifications coexist internally within all of us, and these identifications are called upon differently within various erotic and nonerotic situations, depending on what is at stake psychically.

Bisexuality, as it has been understood in the psychoanalytic community, has been implicitly pathologized. Despite Freud's (1937) later views, which encompassed a universal psychic bisexuality as the foundation of psychosexual development, bisexual practice remains suspect, undermining as it does the premise of heterosexuality as normative. For those with a pathologizing bent, bisexuality seems to suggest a defensive denial of difference, a failure to resolve infantile fantasies of omnipotence in Fast's (1984) sense, an inability to commit oneself to the reality of gender limits and hence object choice. "In the world of dreams we are all magical, bisexual, and immortal!" (McDougall, 1986, p. 215).

Psychoanalytic revisionists, however, critique the very binaries on which the concepts of masculine/feminine, active/passive rest, thus throwing into question the foundation of the "bi"-ness of "bi"-sexuality (Goldner, 1991). The disputes in theorizing bisexuality parallel the disputes in the butch/femme discourse. Are the categories involved ultimately a reaffirmation of the essentialist dichotomies or a postmodern disruption of locatedness?

Within psychoanalytic parlance, bisexual is usually understood to refer to the wish to be both sexes (or possess the character traits associated with them) rather than the desire to have both sexes. Again, this is the result of counterpoising having and being—the heterosexually constructed opposition between desire and identification. Dispensing with that artificial opposition allows for more than the psychologically veridical occurrence of multigendered identifications and muiltisexual desires.

## on the privileging of genital sex

Within the spectrum of lesbian relationships, there is a romantic but essentially asexual relationship between women that, in this country, has often been referred to as the Boston marriage.

Originating in the late nineteenth century, the Boston marriage offered middle-class, career woman companionship, nurturance, communion of kindred spirits, romance, and undoubtedly—in some (but not all) relationships—sex without the stigma of perversion. According to Faderman, who has done the most extensive research in the area, a Boston marriage in the late nineteenth century offered all the advantages of having a significant other without carrying the burdens of heterosexuality (Faderman, 1981, 1993). But this was essentially before there were lesbians. "Lesbianism" as a circumscribed category of sexuality (as contrasted with the real existence of romantic physical relationships between and among women) was a creation of sexologists writing in the 1870s whose work was not broadly read initially. Hence woman could live together and be "above suspicion." By the 1920s, however, paradigms of sexuality for women had changed; romantic friendships were no longer seen as innocent, and thus were no longer condoned (Faderman, 1993). Moreover, women themselves were forced to question and defend the presence or absence of their sexuality in a way that might once have been unthinkable.

Even today, many long-term lesbian relationships are not particularly genital; others are asexual or barely sexual.[4] The term *Boston marriage*, describing a socially condoned relationship among a particular class of women within a particular culture in a particular moment in history, is also an attempt to create language where there is none for a continuing reality of lesbian life. Faderman suggests that "perhaps the sine qua non of a lesbian relationship is not genital sexuality" p. 40). She, among others, questions the phallocentrically based prescription of sexuality that exists in our particular historiocultural era and asks us to broaden our concept of the meanings and structures of committed love between women (Rich, 1981; Frye, 1990; Hall, 1993; Rothblum & Brehony, 1993). How is it that genital touching becomes the primary signifier of intimacy, they ask?

Marilyn Frye (1990), in a more radical position, challenges the very category of sex as male and heterosexist. She objects to the privileging of penile/vaginal intercourse culminating in orgasm ("doing it") as defining the discourse and hence leaving sensual touching, her sexual domain, outside the realm of legitimate sexuality. According to Frye, the rhythms of lesbian love and passion cannot be mapped on "eight minute" male definitions of sex. She maintains that lesbian sexuality is not encoded by this discourse. There is no linguistic matrix for the experiences of bodily play, tactile communication, the ebb and flow of intense excitement, arousal, tension, release, comfort, discomfort, pain, and pleasure (p. 312). Ultimately, Frye argues, heterosexual intercourse is not synchronous with the ontology of the lesbian body.

## lesbian bed death

Yet, on a parallel but somehow paradoxical plane of the lesbian continuum, we find the phenomenon of "lesbian bed death," one of the most common complaints heard in the consulting room vis-à-vis lesbian sexuality. In or out of the consulting room, in common parlance, *lesbian bed death* refers to the ongoing or impending cessation of genital sexuality as well as other forms of passionate or lustful sexual touching. Lesbian couples often separate or triangulate over what appears to be irreconcilable differences in the expression of sexual desire. Unlike Faderman's (1981) Boston marriage, or the new Boston marriage described by Rothblum and Brehony (1993), women in relationships complaining of "lesbian bed death" mourn the loss of their mutually expressed desire. How does this come to pass?

Not speaking to the issue of "lesbian bed death" per se, but concerned about the lack of ongoing sexuality in mature lesbian relationships, Nichols (1987) suggests that lesbians, like many of their heterosexual sisters, are sexually repressed. She is not using the term in the classical psychoanalytical sense (Freud, 1917), but rather to mean inhibited, constricted, suppressed, or somehow rendered silent and inactive. She enumerates reasons for the falling off of sexuality: the inhibition of anger, internalized homophobia whereby eliminating genital sex demonstrates that one is not really a lesbian, the failure of each of the women to feel comfortable as sexual initiator or aggressor. It is primarily this last inhibition, the reluctance to initiate a sexual encounter, that lesbians share with their heterosexual female counterparts.

What Nichols approaches but does not fully apprehend is that to be a subject of desire rather than its object, and to act agentically in accordance with that subjectivity, stands at odds with one's internalized gender role as a woman. Heterosexual women look to men to release them from this conflict, either by assuming the role of initiator or by bestowing legitimacy on their feminine desirability. For two women, the conflict between agency and internalized gender role can become more paralyzing, especially if it is unknown or unacknowledged.

Issues of sexuality are often conflated with issues of true self (Bollas, 1989; A. Schwartz, 1996). It is perhaps not surprising, then, that lesbians complain of the disappearance of desire: either their own, or as a presence in their relationship.

It has been my clinical experience, however, that what contributes most often to the falling away of passion within lesbian relationships—

and by this I am not privileging genital sex as the signifier of said passion—is an avoidance of intense desire and sexual passion out of a fear of ruthlessness on the part of oneself or one's lover. Bollas (1989) speaks to the issue in presumably heterosexual couples:

> In lovemaking, foreplay begins as an act of relating. Lovers attend to mutual erotic interests. As the economic factor increases, this element of lovemaking will recede somewhat (though not disappear) as the lovers surrender to that ruthlessness inherent in erotic excitement. This ruthlessness has something to do with a joint loss of consciousness, a thoughtlessness which is incremental to erotic intensity. It is a necessary ruthlessness as both lovers destroy the relationship in order to plunge into a reciprocal orgasmic use. Indeed the destruction of relationship is itself pleasurable and the conversion of relating to using transforms ego libido into increased erotic drive. If a couple cannot assume this essential destructiveness, erotic intensity may not give in to mutual orgasms. Instead, reparation may be the fundamental exchange between such couples with partners entering into prolonged mother-child scenarios, of cuddling, holding, or soothing. This may be because such persons have not been able to experience a good destruction of the object, and reparative work is activated during the arrival of instinctual urges. When this happens, sexual uses of the object may be enacted as dissociated activities. Instead lovers may masturbate each other, with one partner relating to the other's sexual needs and mothering them through it, or at an extreme, in the perverse act, the couple may wear interesting garments and introduce curious acts to entirely split off the destructive side of erotic life in a kind of performance art. (pp. 26–27)

I would take issue with Bollas in the universalizing of his theory. The absence of genital sex, mutual and or singular orgasms in the presence of sensual and erotic touching does not always signal a problem of desire/true self. Similarly, I would argue that gender performance is intrinsic to many forms of sexuality rather than prima facie evidence of its dissociation. Only a lesbian couple can make a diagnosis of their bed death with the pathology thus implied. It is the falling away of their sexuality, whatever its form. With the decentering of the phallocentrically derived privileging of genital sex, lesbians reconstruct their sexuality to include a spectrum of relationships and expressions of desire.

However, it is interesting to note that Bollas's discussion of truth and the place of ruthlessness in lovemaking comes in the context of a larger discussion of true self and object usage. Although theoretically Winnicott's (1971) distinction between object relating and object usage has a developmental tilt (with the former preceding the latter), I would suggest that, within lesbian couples, the difficulty with ruthlessness is not so much a function of a basic fault, so to speak, but of a fear/ avoidance of the emergence of wanton and capacious subjectivity. A seeming requirement of ruthlessness, the consequent negation of the Other, even temporarily, is associated with a male/aggressive subjectivity so consciously eschewed in segments of lesbian culture.

Lesbian couples who seek therapeutic help often seem to have difficulty incorporating healthy competition and aggression into their ongoing relationship (Lindenbaum, 1985). This suppression of aggression, the avoidance of ruthlessness, manifests as a diminution or deadening of the couple's libido. If acted out, a triangulation might occur both as an expression of one partner's anger and unconscious wish to resuscitate the passion by means of jealousy, possessiveness, and a legitimization by way of a hurtful retaliation.

## to conclude

Psychoanalytic theory has been based on both the confluence of and the opposition of gender identification and object choice. Lesbian sexuality as theorized or practiced does not appear to be. Erotically, being and desiring a woman do not stand in a relationship of synecdoche. Lesbian eroticism is more aptly a confluence of multiple identifications and positions of desire.

Notions of overinclusive matrices of depathologized gender identifications/representations (Fast, 1984; Bassin, 1997) can help us understand the incorporation of phallic imagery within some expressions of lesbian sexuality without it signifying exclusive male identifications or signs of "masculine protest."

Lesbian eroticism as read by intention, unconscious fantasy, and practice calls into question the presumed essentialist connections of biology, gender, and sexuality. Lesbian sexuality and/or multisexuality, can be read as resistance to fixed identities of gender role and object choice. Once positions of identification and desire are disrupted, once heterosexuality is removed as the underpinning of gender identification (Butler, 1995), then we are jettisoned from a classic psychoanalytic space into a queer universe of polymorphous diversity. Lesbian sexuality questions the privileging of genital sex and the equation of appropriate gender attribution with mature sexuality. Lesbian sexuality as theorized and practiced suggests an eroticism that allows for multiple identifications, multiple positions of desire and objects, to reflect a polymorphously diverse sexuality.

Finally, lesbian eroticism is about gender performance (Butler, 1990a, b), the performative creation of a multiplicity of genders that more accurately signal individually fluent sexual desires and temperament.

Clinical psychoanalysis is uniquely situated to traverse a universe of mature sexualities (not a priori an infantile/undifferentiated libido) that is responsive to and desirous of a variety of sexual objects having differing but not necessarily contradictory internal resonances with a variety of early object relations.

Clinical psychoanalysis, then, is uniquely situated to traverse the queer universe.

## notes

1. For a review of the sexuality debates of the 1980s within the feminist community, see Bar On (1992). For a more biased but humorous account of "sexually incorrct" (SI) sex, see Nichols (1987).

2. For a fascinating discussion of clothes and gender, see Garber (1992).

3. For reference to sado-masochistic practice see Samois (1981); and Linden, Pagano, Russell, & Star, (1982). For the new Boston marriage, see Rothblum, & Brehony, (1993).

4. In a study by Phillip Blumstein and Pepper Schwarz (1983), only one-third of the couples in relationships of at least two years' duration had sex once a week or more, compared to two-thirds of their heterosexual counterparts. Sex is not defined. Almost half the lesbians in long-term relationsips of ten years or more had sex less than once a month, compared to 15 percent of their heterosexual counterparts. (Pepper and Schwartz, 1983, p. 196). Pepper and Schwartz also reported that lesbians interviewed preferred nongenital contact such as hugging and cuddling to genital sex. Lesbians also seem to have oral sex less frequently.

# the gendered self . . . a question of subjectivities

if I come into a room out of the sharp misty light
and hear them talking a dead language
if they ask me my identity
what can I say but
I am the androgyne
I am the living mind you fail to describe
in your dead language
the lost noun, the verb surviving
only in the infinitive
the letters of my name are written under the lids
of the newborn child

—Rich, *"The Stranger"*

What would have to happen in the so-called psychoanalytic community for an ethos to be created
in which patients were encouraged to mourn the
loss of all their repressed gender identities?

—Phillips, *"Keep It Moving"*

The construction of coherence conceals the gender discontinuities that run rampant within heterosexual, bisexual, and gay and lesbian contexts in
which gender does not seem to follow form sex,
and desire or sexuality generally, does not seem to
follow from gender; indeed, where none of these
dimensions of significant corporeality "express" or
reflect one another.

—Butler, *"Gender Trouble"*

The notion of a gendered identity and the experience of a gendered self have been integral to the ways in which our culture thinks about women and men, and to the difficulties *some* have (those we meet in the consulting room, rather than those we do not) with themselves. Advertising and other media within the commercial world often play to gender anxieties, proffering various products with the idea that they will guarantee or enhance the manliness/femininity of the targeted consumer.

For people labeled or self-identified as gay, lesbian, bisexual, the issue of gender is often problematic. Most commonly throughout our culture, there is a conflation of gender and sexuality. Gay men are not "real men"; lesbians are not "real women" (Isay, 1989; Magee & Miller, 1992; Corbett, 1993; O'Connor & Ryan, 1993). Within psychoanalytic and psychotherapeutic practice, difficulties arise when there is either a perceived or experienced discordance among varied self-representations and/or the perceptions and attribution of gender evaluations from others. She is . . . I am . . . , "too masculine," "not feminine enough," "not a real girl," "too butch," "too femme," "throw like a girl," "a tomboy," "a man trapped in a woman's body."

Within the psychoanalytic world there has been a slow but steady revolution brewing in the ways in which we analyze and conceptualize gender (Dimen, 1991; Goldner, 1991; Harris, 1991; Benjamin, 1995;

Bassin, 1997). Informed by postmodern/poststructuralist critiques (Foucault, 1978, 1980; Butler, 1990a) we ask whether we really need to keep on "doing sex and gender" as we have in the past—that is, do sex and gender necessarily have a mimetic relation to each other?

More disruptive questions come to mind. Is a fixed, discrete, or coherent *gendered* sense of self intrinsic to our experience of actualized well-being? Does that gendered sense self have to correspond to some "objective reality" about the *sexed* body? Are there constitutive constraints that are relative here? Is there a "real" body onto which we superimpose meaning, or does the meaning construct the body itself?

## psychoanalysis constructs gender

Once Freud's "talking cure" had painted an inexorable path to the forgotten/repressed psychosexual world of childhood as the primary source of our psychic ills, the artful "science" of psychoanalysis embarked upon a project to elaborate a universal developmental schema that would be true to the phenomenology of our patients' conscious experience as well as to their unconscious manifestations as reconstructed through dreams, fantasy, association, and enactment. [And although numerous critics have railed against Freud and psychoanalysis as perpetrators of a theory that seemed to reify the woman's place as subordinate in the gender hierarchy, it has been psychoanalysis first and foremost, like modern feminist theory, that has identified gender as a primary category upon which culture rests (A. Schwartz, 1984a).]

Within classical psychoanalysis, there have been attempts to revise Freud's (1925, 1931) basic schema of psychosexual development, which combines a stark phallocentricity with a conflation of sexuality and gender identity. For example, Tyson (1982) both alters the timeline for certain stages of development and, more importantly, rejects Freud's thesis that girls' earliest sexuality is "masculine"/clitoral/active and must be rejected for a femininity that is vaginal/passive.[1] Tyson's model is based on fixed biological sex attribution at birth, followed by overlapping sequences of emergent gender definition. She begins with a gradually elaborated delineation of body image as a function of oral, anal, urethral, and genital activities, which take place in a matrix of maternal interactions. Genital arousal stimulates an awareness of the anatomical distinction between the sexes (read primarily as penis/no penis) so that by the middle of the second year major body representations are formed. It is at this time that the core gender identity—that is, the primary sense of being male or female, belonging to one sex or the other—is established (Stoller, 1968). If all goes well during the so-called phallic phase, the girl faces and largely resolves her increased ambivalence toward her mother (read penis/no penis) and ultimately learns to value her body and her femininity, reinforcing her earlier identification with a maternal ego ideal.

Tyson differentiates core gender identity from gender role, which she defines as overt behavior in relationships with other people vis-à-vis gender, and gender-role identity, the sum of conscious and unconscious mental representations of dialogues with other people vis-à-vis one's gender identity as well as identification with role models.

Core gender identity, traditionally thought to be a bedrock of essential mental health (that is, its absence has been a marker of psychosis and other serious personality disturbances) is actually more about understanding categories and attaining mastery of the linguistic ordering of culture. Acknowledging this distinction, Benjamin (1995) substitutes the notion of "nominal gender identification," which recognizes that knowing that one belongs to one sex or the other doesn't obviate multiple identifications. In this way, core gender identity, or nominal gender identification is related to mental health, if mental health is seen as an accession to prevailing cultural norms. The obverse then raises the problematic of whether the refusal to accede to cultural norms renders one mentally ill.

The concept of gender role identity, then, suggests more clearly a gendered sense of self that is multiply determined by biological, sociological, and psychological facets. Gender role identity involves an internal self-evaluation of maleness or femaleness and is thus continuous rather than discrete, mutable in a way that a core or nominal gender identity is not. It has to do with meanings of being in a female or male body and is developed in the context of object relations (A. Schwartz, 1986).

The unitary basis of the concept, however, points out that which is relatively fixed and enduring, and is in contradiction to the phenomenology of our experience. The notion of gender role *identities* speaks more closely to the construct of gender as we live it and allows for the uneasy coexistence of concepts of gender both as a function of performance and of internal representations of gendered object relations.

Tyson stresses the separation of gender and sexuality and emphasizes that sexual partner orientation, as she terms it, has its roots not in gender but in pre-oedipal and oedipal object relations, the libidinal vagaries in the oscillation of cathexes between mother and father. Since sexuality and gender are not totally conflated, theoretically, her schema allows for a feminine woman who chooses another feminine woman for her love object, though this is not the way in which classical psychoanalysts traditionally see the evolution of female homosexuality nor is it what, most likely, Tyson had in mind.

Clinically her timetable is consistent with later work that points to the difficulties that may arise when conflicts around attachment are coincident with the child's gaining the appurtenances of gender (A. Schwartz, 1984, 1986; Coates, et. al, 1991). Conceptually, Tyson's sequence is problematical in that it reifies a binary system of gender, where feeling/behaving/identifying as female or male becomes a developmental achievement. Like any model emerging from a one-person psychology, this schema does not adequately allow for the greater psychic prevalence of our multiply gendered representations and the myriad part and whole and object relations on which they are based.

As Mitchell (1992) points out, once we discard the strict biological determinism that emanates from classical drive theory, then the *meaning* of bodies and body parts and bodily experience derives from the mutually regulatory, interpersonal, linguistic, and cultural matrix into which a person is born. Thus the anal, genital, urethral sensations of which Tyson speaks, far from being biologically constitutive, are lived bodily experiences that can only take shape as they emerge from an interpersonal agar.

Some feminist revisionists (Dinnerstein, 1977; Chodorow, 1978; Spieler, 1986) have attempted to show how it is that certain aspects of female gender-role identity are reproduced within the culture, others (Benjamin, 1988, 1995) have pointed out how limited our conception of girls' identificatory processes are. Relational theorists, informed by postmodernism, have attempted to critique the very notion of gender as it appears as a psychoanalytic and a cultural category.

The relational theorists emphasize that gender develops in and through relationships with others (Mitchell, 1988, 1991). Discarding the constraints of a one-person psychology and viewing gender from what she terms a systemic relational perspective, Goldner (1991) reminds us that cultural fantasies about gender shape the familial expectations, relationship patterns, and injunctions that mold the internalized system of gender relations out of which the self grows. She contests the privileging of a unified psychic world and questions the coherence, consistency, and conformity of a unified identity by positioning the acquisition of gender identity as a problem as well as a solution. A unified, coherent, nondiscordant gender identity entails the defensive inhibition of cross-gender identification, which in turn requires the splitting off or disavowal of gender-incongruent thoughts, acts, and impulses. One might well ask whether this is to be viewed as a developmental accomplishment. Dimen, a relational theorist who defines gender as difference and difference as the paradoxical space that selfhood inhabits, astutely characterizes the problematic relationship between gender and selfhood as a function of the "contemporaneous crystallization in development . . . [ which] . . . makes them seem, indeed feel, joined at the heart" (1991, p. 337). Whether one adheres more closely to Mahler's (Mahler, et. al, 1975) developmental model of separation-individuation, or to Stern's (1985) model of the emerging self—the interweaving of self and other—the vagaries of attachment and separation provide fertile ground for conflations and confusions with regard to the gendered self.

Explorations of self and identity form the crux of much of psychoanalytic practice. Concomitantly, ideas and fantasies about the self are key in the phenomenology of identities, but they should not be confused with something that actually exists (Grossman, 1982, 1991; Ogden, 1989). The concept of a unified self is a fantasy that can play a central role in organizing and integrating experience.[2] Psychically then, the self is an organizational construct, a variegated, multisurfaced composite of object representations and relations of which gender is a major but not necessarily predominate component (Mitchell, 1991; Grosz, 1994).

## what's happened to the body?

From Freud, standard bearer in a quixotic way of the modern age, to the relational theorists, informed as they are by the feminist postmodern, psychoanalysis has come a long way. Anatomy is no longer destiny. Moreover, there appears to be a danger of losing the body altogether.

If we disrupt the relation of sex and gender, bodies and sex, so that we challenge the very nature of those categories and the foundation of their attribution, then the modern world of Freud is drastically upended—as it has been. Freud's original project—to map out the developmental interplay between psyche and soma—has been undermined by the deconstruction of the constitutional component of the allegedly biologically given soma. Such upending allows provocateurs like Butler (1993a) to query whether, in a given instance, if a man's primary identification is with his mother and if through that identification he desires another man, then is that desire to be classified as homo or heteroerotic?

From a somewhat different perspective, Zita (1992) attempts to illustrate the debate between the modern/essentialist and postmodern positions on gender/sex identities centering on the body, using a philosophical analysis of the claim to legitimacy by male lesbians. In these scattered instances within the lesbian feminist community, men claim to actually *be* lesbians, rather than think, act, or feel *like* lesbians. How are we to understand that?

If, according to some postmodernists, the body is itself a product of cultural discourse, what prevents a male body from occupying the positionality of "woman" or "lesbian" (Suleiman, 1986; Butler, 1990a)? How does any body, even one with an XX sex chromosome and primary sex characteristics identified as female, become a woman? What makes any sex or gender identity real, Suleiman asks, and when it is possible that humans make up these meanings through the disciplinary practice of "doing gender" or "having sex"?

In the 1970s some lesbians sought to shift the definition of lesbian from one that was sexually based to one that was founded on politics. Hence, a woman claimed a lesbian identity not by virtue of her sexual fantasies or actual sexual behavior with another woman, but by disengaging from the "domination of the heteropatriarchy" (Radicalesbians, 1973, p. 111). Couldn't a male lay claim to such a position of disengagement?

For a modernist, this male is of necesseity mistaken; the identity as lesbian is affixed to a certain kind of body, biologically determined and correspondingly labeled female. This binary is universal. The presence or absence of certain anomalies (discrepancies between chromosomal, hormonal, and gonadal sex types, hermaphroditism, and so forth) within the species does not seem to affect the basic binary system of sex assignment. (Foucault, 1978). For by whatever criteria one attempts to define a lesbian—political, conscious or unconscious fantasy, overt sexual behavior, assumed identification with a certain community—there will always be persons who "don't fit."

The question thus becomes: are these categories of sex, gender, and identity, naturalist in basis, or socially constructed and inscribed upon a range of human feelings and behaviors? How do we understand the myriad situations in which there is a discordance between self-attribution and the attribution of categories made by others? Doesn't that discordance suggest the questioning of the meaningfulness or validity of the categories themselves? Transsexuals seek to change the physical structure of their bodies in order to have greater consistency in the readings of their sex and gender identities, while transgendered individuals claim that their very existence calls into question traditional readings of morphology and the fixedness of sex identity as located solely within body (Feinberg, 1993). Female impersonators, drag kings and queens all call the gender/sex categories to task through parody and performance.

Is the existence of these discordances, however, sufficient to warrant the abandonment of the notion of a material body that transcends the vagaries of cultural discourse? Susan Bordo (1990), in a compelling essay on gender skepticism (the critique of gender as an analytic category), challenges what she terms the postmodern "dream of everywhere," an epistemological perspective free of the locatedness and the limitations of embodied existence. For Bordo, the postmodern images of "cyborgs" or "tricksters" indicate a resistance to the recognition that one is always *somewhere*:[3]

> To deny the unity and stability of identity is one thing. The epistemological fantasy of *becoming* multiplicity—the dream of limitless multiple embodiments, allowing one to dance from place to place and self to self—is another. What sort of body is it that is free to change its shape and location at will, that can become anyone and travel everywhere? If the body is no body is a metaphor for our locatedness in space and time, and this for the finitude of human perception and knowledge, then the postmodern body is no body at all. (Bordo, 1990, p. 145)

Bordo accurately points out the fallacy of confusing a critique of gender as a totalizing construct (and perhaps mistakenly valorizing that aspect of one's identity over, race, class, ethnicity, sexuality) with its very elimination as a viable category at all. She states emphatically to the poststructuralist deconstructionists that the dream of escape from human locatedness is a fantasy—the dream of being everywhere.

Do we need to place the constructedness and materiality of the body on irreducibly opposite poles? Butler (1993a) points out, as does Bassin (1996), that for Freud (1923) the ego is first and foremost a bodily ego, a boundaried sense of self springing from projections or mental images of bodily sensations. But Butler eschews a causal temporality between the body and the idea of the body. She argues that the body is not prior to the idea of the body: "If erotogenicity is produced through the conveying of a bodily activity through an idea, then the idea and the conveying are phenomenologically coincident. As a result, it would not be possible to speak about a body part that precedes and gives rise to an idea, for it is the idea that emerges spontaneously with the phenomenologically accessible body, indeed that guarantees its accessibility" (Butler, 1993a, p. 59).

Once the physical body and the idea of that body become enmeshed, we are left swimming in a miasma of cultural inscriptions and their permeation in and through our experience of our bodily selves. The claim that the body is not prior to the idea of the body, nor that it is impossible to partial out the body from the idea of the body, does not reduce the body to an idea. Hence, we return to the sex/gendering of lived bodies in an object world, not as the determining sign but as one aspect of what Grosz terms embodied subjectivity, psychical corporeality (1994, p. 22).[4]

For Freud (1925), in the modern world, anatomy *was* destiny, morphology described and circumscribed psychosexual gendered development. In the postmodern world, there is no "pre-cultural, pre-social, or pre-linguistic pure body," the body is a "social and discursive object, a body bound up in the order of desire, signification, and power" (Grosz, 1994, p. 19).

Although Grosz maintains that the body, as much as the psyche or subject, can be regarded as a cultural and historical product, she does recognize the constitutive constraints of its biological limits and capacities. Women develop breasts and menstruate, they have a clitoris and vagina. They have sexed bodies different from those bodies that have penises, testes, produce sperm. Like Freud, Grosz sees the body as the heart of the psyche. It is to these lived bodies in interaction with other embodied subjectivities that psychological and sociocultural meanings adhere.

### gendered selves

From a relational perspective, then, it is clear that our sense of our gendered selves and the bodies they inhabit are given meaning and connotation as a function of social intercourse. We are not gendered in isolation, but in relation to significant objects and the cultural/linguistic matrix into which we are born (Mitchell, 1992). Gender-role identity, then, is partly a function of who we are in relation to that other object—a relation subject to many interactions, interpretations, and also fantasies. Thus, I would suggest that a relational perspective to internalized gender-role identities inevitably leads to an understanding of multiple genders and multiple gendered relations both in fantasy and performance.

This is a large psychic leap from one of a unified, coherent, and consistent gender identity based on a complex process of internalization and identification. However, from a clinical and theoretical perspective, it is important, as Benjamin suggests (1995), not to throw out the baby of identification as an internal psychic process with the bath water of identity as a reified thing. Rather than abandoning a developmental approach, Benjamin suggests that psychoanalysis needs to decenter and refigure stagelike theories so that phases need not be critical nor subsume other phases.

Loewald (1973), writing on the process of internalization, also suggests that "early levels of psychic development are not simply outgrown and left behind but continue to be active, at least intermittently, during later life including adulthood. They coexist, although overshadowed by later developmental stages, with later stages and continue to have their impact on them" (pp. 81–82). Loewald acknowledges that identifications are often only "way-stations" on the road to more complex internal psychic structures. Identifications, though necessary as preliminary phases, to the extent to which the unending process of internalization succeeds, are dissolved and destroyed internally, and something novel comes into being. Thus, for Loewald, in identification there is an erasure of difference, an merging of subject and object. It is a stepping-stone to internalization, but in internalization there is a redifferentiation, an emancipation from the object, the creation of an enriched psychic structure in which the mimetic identity with the object is renounced.

There is no mention of gender here. But in Loewald's model, one can see the possibility for the transitional space in which gender plays: the splits, incorporations of part objects, the multiple identifications that later theory suggests (Dimen, 1991). In a similar vein, Butler (1990a) offers that gendered subjectivity may be understood as a history of identifications in which gender identities emerge and sexual desires shift and vary so that different identifications come into play depending upon given intrapersonal contexts and cultural opportunities.

As psychoanalysts, we are interested not only in how representations are organized but also in what determines their entrance into the internal world. According to Stern (1989), representations are of relational patterns, cumulative interactive histories, a series of repetitive interactive events that are mutually derived though subjectively constructed. They are a function of both objective events and subjective experiences. The work of Stern and others (Beebe, 1986) alerts us to the minute and omnipresent feedback system originating in earliest infancy between the caretakers and the child and how it extends with greater complexity as the child matures and her surrounding system changes. The parameters of the feedback loop will vary, of course, in the intensity and focus of the subjective experience, given both the immediate and the developmental needs of the child; and they covary as they mesh with the particulars of the mothering relationship within a given developmental period (A. Schwartz, 1993).

It is easily within the realm of extrapolation, then, that encoded in the empathic and recognition responses of the interactions will be megabytes of information about the mothering one's conscious and unconscious feelings about separation and autonomy; bodily competence and jouissance in its broadest sense; aggression; and, of course, sex and gender roles. The key parameters of these various interactions, repeated in a consistent and continuous fashion, are experienced and stored first kinesthetically or proprioceptively, and ultimately, with the advent of language, they may be internalized and symbolically represented. There is no need in this model for gender to assume hegemony over identity formation. But it does allow for the peculiarities of culture specificity where the parameter of gender might well be, as it is in our culture, among the primary organizers of identity as it is culled from significant others.

Gender assumptions and projections made by parents vary significantly within the first twenty-four hours of an infant's life (Rubin et. al., 1974).[5] Hence, one may expect that attitudes and "information" about gender (arising from the various meanings of maleness and femaleness to the caretakers—the valence of sameness and difference, for example) form a major component of the feedback loop. Internal working models of relationships will be organized around conscious and unconscious familial "information" as it is transmitted by and experiences living with various attachment/caretaking figures.[6] Thus, an integral part of the feedback loop will be the conscious and unconscious attitudes and feelings about gendered selves that are then incorporated into the nascent internalized object world.

As it becomes possible to understand gendered subjectivity as the culmination of a history of internalized interactions—which do not of necessity imply an unbending internal coherence (Butler, 1990a)—it becomes possible to understand cross-gender identifications as normative rather than pathogomonic.

Identifying with caretakers of both sexes as a function of internalizing aspects of repetitive interaction, the child begins to symbolize genital meanings and unconsciously to assimilate the gestures, behavior, and vocabulary supplied by the culture to express masculinity and femininity. Psychoanalytic theorists (Aron, 1995; Benjamin, 1995; Bassin, 1996) have begun to see the ability to represent and symbolize the role of the other, consequent to the conscious or preconscious access to cross-gender identifications, as contributing to creativity and hence as leading to personal expansion rather than necessarily to pain and suffering.

Bassin (1996) has written most extensively about this and defines the more mature female mind as overinclusive, by which she means identification with opposite-sexed parents based on early body-ego experiences:[7] "The physical impossibility of cross-sex behavior does not prevent the mind from playing with reality, symbolizing, creating imaginative and empathic identifications. Symbols serve as intrapsychic bridges over rigid gender polarities, and help the self reconcile the dilemma of bisexuality . . . without recourse to repression or perversion" (pp. 24–25).

In Bassin's schema, there is a body-ego experience that is both differentiated *and* overinclusive. She locates two strands of development: one moves toward a firm gender identity based on identification with the same-sexed parent, and the other simultaneously allows the psyche to move away from the containing limitations of gender based on an early, overinclusive, body-ego experience with early nongenitaled parents in order to form identifications with parents of the "opposite" sex. Bassin's theory unfortunately assumes heterosexual dual parenting and implies heterosexual orientation.

However, I see what Bassin suggests as mature female genital development—that is, the optimal transcendence of sexual polarities and rigid gender identities—to be very much like what lesbians do and often worry about: that is, they use overinclusive body-ego symbolizations, often phallic in their sexual fantasies and gender performance. The use of such symbolizations does not necessarily reflect a femaleness gone askew but rather a "flexible female organization [which] facilitates the mourning of lost omnipotence by identification and imaginative elaboration through symbolization . . . The mastery and symbolic use of cross-sex identifications contributes to the ability to play beyond the gender-normative structures, as in the musician's ability to improvise after mastering basic musical techniques" (Bassin, 1996, p. 187).

Basic musical techniques in this instance would be understood as a core gender identity, the nonpsychotic acceptance of the constitutive constraints of the body and the sex that the culture has ascribed to that body. "In this context, one can know but supersede the reality of one's gender-specific identifications, as a jazz musician can play with time, or as a dancer must respect gravity and space but is not tied to them" (Bassin, 1996, p. 187).

### clinical note

Marta feels bad in her body sometimes, heavy and fat. When she feels bad in her body she feels that she is bad. Marta's parents separated when she was eleven months old. At age two she went to live with her grandparents who lived nearby her Midwestern city. Mother, a busy professional, came to visit on weekends and took Marta back in her home when she remarried and Marta was six. Marta loved her mother fiercely and was devastated at her death when Marta was eleven. She recalls being weighed compulsively almost every day during the times that she lived with her mother and having her diet monitored stringently both at home and at school.

Marta is a lesbian who feels that she should have been a boy, and who has internalized her mother's reflected feelings about her own body. As a child, Marta's body was both abandoned and invasively controlled. Marta has had the fleeting fantasy that she has lost her penis and has a "memory" of her grandmother making a slip one day in talking to the child, prefacing a sentence with "when you had a penis."

This clinical material is offered not because it is typical of lesbians or because it is connected to any universal process of lesbian sexuality or identity, but rather because it illustrates the sometimes painful conflation of body-ego functions and gender that occurs in this woman whose bad/self bad/body woman as abject self is clearly associated with her relation to mother as rejected object.

As an embodied lesbian, Marta's sexuality is not problematic. She enjoys her phallic fantasies but gains sexual pleasure and feels desired as a woman as well. She draws upon her validations by other relations— her grandfather who doted on her, her grandmother to whom she was the special grandchild.

For Marta, the phallus is about issues of power and desirability, of wanting and being wanted. Marta's initial abandonments during her second year coincided with the emergence of her subjective self and beginnings of her abilities to symbolize (Stern, 1985).

During one session, Marta commented that she had been eating more, feeling fat, feeling bad. She was particularly dismayed because it had been Marta's impression that she had been losing weight (Marta never consciously dieted) and perhaps had been eating on purpose even though she was not thinking about it as a way of rebelling against her mother (and analyst, we may presume!). Marta had always been an extremely obedient child, except that she had not wanted to wear dresses and even, at age four or five, had completely refused to do so. Her next association was to dolls, which she thoroughly rejected, though she loved stuffed animals. Marta has an extensive collection to this day—stuffed animals are not gendered and hence give her more freedom of play.

For Marta, her fat body is a bad body, is her hungry girl's body, is a body not liked by mother—a body to hurt, to damage by alcohol and drugs during adolescence, another time of gender valence (A. Schwartz, 1986). A fat body is a body that calls out for people to look at it and turn away. In the beginning phases of analysis, Marta would plead from the couch, "Don't look at me," by which I understood her desperate need to be seen. Marta's is a body with large breasts and hips that was psychically and physically rejected by a mother who "left" her daughter at age 11 on the cusp of menarche.

And finally, Marta's fat bad body is also a body free of her mother's control, a defiant and hence powerful body, at once a failed woman's body and a phallic body—a large and powerful not-mother's body.

Marta is not clinically obese, nor does she have an eating disorder. Her self-proclaimed healthiest functioning comes when she experiences herself as a big woman constitutionally, big-boned with a large frame, whose real power comes from her agency. She is a lesbian who very much wants to give birth to a baby and who wears men's shoes, as they are the only ones that really fit comfortably.

### quick Q&A

Q: *At the beginning of this chapter, we asked if a fixed, discrete, coherent, gendered sense of self is essential to a sense of well-being. Well, is it?*

A: Gender-disjunctive identities often get repressed, split off, not integrated, disavowed in a culture of gender binaries. This can lead to severe constriction of character, gender performance, sexual exploration, and creative symbolization. Thus, the disavowal of multiplicities of gender representations and identifications required to form such a fixed sense of gender would seem to lead to a constricted psychic life.

Q: *Must a gendered sense of self correspond to the objective reality of the sexed body?*

A: The postmodern position is that the body is a product of cultural discourse.

Q: *Does that mean that we are all tricksters, that there are male lesbians?*

A: The issue is not one of gender/sexual anomalies, or of the denial of constitutive constraints on the physical body, but rather of the impossibility of a material body that lies outside the cultural determined linguistic discourse. As Butler (1993) suggests, if one disrupts the causality between the body and the idea of the body so that one does not take precedence over the other, then we are left with an embodied subjectivity of which gender is one, but not obviously the sole, parameter.

Q: *Why do you continue to distinguish between nominal gender identity and gender role identities?*

A: I think it's an important clinical distinction. Nominal gender identity involves a fundamental awareness of the categories of sex attribution in our culture and the ways in which the culture sees his/her body fitting into those categories. Attitudes toward that fit seem to be important, with the use of patent denial and delusion indicating greater psychic distress. Gender-role identities involve unconscious processes of internalization as a function of our relations with significant gendered others, as well as biological and tempermental factors (Flax, 1996).

Q: *So as to the gendered self . . .*

A: I would prefer to speak of gendered subjectivities that I see as a constantly evolving processing of our histories of internalized interactions; it is a concept that allows for cross-gender, transgendered, and same-sex identifications within a complex, nonlinear matrix of gendered selves and others.

## notes

1. During the psychoanalytic debates of the 1920s and 1930s, Jones (1927), Horney (1924, 1926, 1933), and Klein (1928), among others, took issue with Freud in their belief in a primary femininity for girls, based in part on sensations arising from her vagina.

2. For a further discussion of self, its temporal versus spatial aspects, and issues of authenticity, see "coming out/being heard" in this volume.

3. Donna Haraway (1990) defined a cyborg as a hybrid of machine and organism, a creature of fiction that is created as a function of imagination and material reality, a creature of the postgendered world. Smith-Rosenberg's (1985) tricskter is a creature of indeterminate sex and changeable gender who continually alters her/his body, creates and recreates a personality, and floats across time from period to period, place to place (p. 291).

4. Grosz (1994) insists that there is no *body* as such, only *bodies*, and that in their specificity of field there are other equally important signifiers: racial, cultural, and class particularities.

5. In this study, male and female infants with no significant difference in their Apgar scores were described very differently. Girls were seen by their parents to be "little . . . beautiful . . . delicate . . . weak . . . and resembling their mothers"; whereas the day-old boys were described as "firm . . . more alert . . . stronger . . . and better coordinated." (Rubin, G., Provenzano, F., & Luria, Z., 1974, p. 515).

6. Bowlby (1973, 1980) suggested that the coherence, stability, and substance of relationships are represented by the internalized structures, which he termed internal working models of attachment. It is through these models that individuals are able to perceive, plan, and act in the world. Expanding upon Bowlby, Main, Kaplan, and Cassidy (1985) suggested that "internal working models of relationships also will provide rules for the direction and organization of attention and memory, rules that permit or limit the individual's access to certain forms of knowledge regarding the self, the attachment figure, and the relationship between the self and the attachment figure. These rules will be reflected in the organization of thought and language as it relates directly and indirectly to attachment" (p. 77).

7. Bassin (1996) uses this term very differently from Fast (1984). Fast views overinclusiveness as a function of pre-odipal omnipotence on the part of both boys and girls, which must be worked through and divested in order to appropriate gender identities to form. See "it's a queer universe" in this volume, for additional reference to Fast's work.

# generativity redux*

Generativity, we said, encompasses procreativity, productivity, and creativity, and thus the generation of new beings as well as of new products and new ideas, including a kind of self-generation concerned with further identity development.
—ERIKSON, *"The Life Cycle Completed"*

A woman's reproductive capacity shapes her life.
—CHASSEGUET-SMIRGEL, *"The Consideration of Some Blind Spots"*

This is Heather. She lives in a little house with a big apple tree in the front yard and lots of tall grass in the back yard. Heather's favorite number is two. She has two arms, two legs, two eyes, two ears, two hands and two feet. Heather also has two pets: a ginger colored cat named Gingersnap and a big black dog named midnight. Heather also has two mommies: Mama Jane and Mama Kate.
—NEWMAN, *Heather Has Two Mommies*

*An earlier, somewhat related version of the first half of this paper appeared in *Psychoanalysis and Psychotherapy, 11* (1), pp. 25–33 (1994).

## femininity as motherhood

Classical psychoanalysis has long conflated motherhood with femininity. Whether female identity was a development secondary to a universal phallic monism (Freud, 1925, 1931) or was considered more essential in its psychosexual roots (Jones, 1927; Horney, 1933), the achievement of heterosexuality and fantasies of impregnation were seen as inevitable outcomes of the successful negotiation of the oedipal stage and were hence the bedrock of the "feminine core" (Deutsch, 1925).

Thus the generativity of women was equated with mothering, which itself was equated with femininity cum heterosexuality. One of the tasks of psychoanalysis in the 1920s was to explain how it was that some women stray off the "path" (enough to cause major consternation, it would seem), reject this developmental equation of femininity/heterosexuality, and with it, the fulfillment of generative dreams through domesticity and maternal bliss (Freud, 1920; Horney, 1926).

If one is not a mother and has not the desire to be, then one's femininity is at risk. If one lives in a culture that affirms the gender binary as the foundation of meaningful person categories, then how as a gender "misfit" does one gain the internal legitimacy that allows for generativity—here defined as the purposeful extension of self to others, the prideful passing on of me to you—within a relationship of care?

For lesbians in particular, the bars to generativity are external as well as internal. The state-sanctioned homophobia operative in the work arena makes it difficult for lesbians to mentor with any degree of authenticity. Internally, the continual erosion of self esteem through the questioning of gender and sexual orientation ripples and distorts the surface of recognition requisite for the self-affirmation intrinsic to generativity.

Freud (1925, 1931) views mothering as the route to heterosexuality rather than an as end in itself. Penis envy, the ghost in the maternity machine, is ushered in by "the shock" of discovering the anatomical difference between the sexes and the girl's consequent dismay at her obviously inferior organ. The shock of the sexual difference, coupled with masturbatory taboos, initiates the beginnings of a torturous and circumlocutory route to heterosexuality, where the wish for a baby becomes the linchpin. "She gives up her wish for a penis and puts in place of it a wish for a child; and it is with that purpose in view that she takes her father as love-object. Her mother becomes the object of her jealousy" (Freud, 1925, p. 256). Narcissistic reparation for the "lack," visited upon her by her mother, can be made up by the oedipal girl by renouncing mother as her love object and taking father instead. Mother is no longer a libidinal object but rather an object of identification.

Freud (1931) recognized that this was a path not so eagerly followed by many, and that psychoanalysts had grossly underestimated both the intensity of the attachment between little girls and their mothers and the concomitant eroticism (Wrye & Welles, 1994). Thus, in theory, we are left with this strange situation whereby the desire for a baby rests on the renunciation of active clitoral (homo) sexuality, or acceptance of a passive "vaginal" femininity that is implicitly heterosexual. According to classical theory, in normative development, the little girl is to give up her "masculine," clitoral sexuality in favor of her so-called feminine, passive self. She will not *have* her mother: she will *become* her instead. (Jones, 1927).

Thus—notes the paradox—women as mothers are not necessarily fulfilling their generative needs but rather their narcissistic ones, repairing an alleged injury through displacement. Similarly, women who choose to pursue career ambitions have felt, until the second wave of feminism, that they must cede all claims to motherliness, if not mothering per se (Benedek, 1973). The paths to devaluation have been manifold for women: a heterosexual woman who is "just a mother" and "only a housewife" chafes at her oft-diminished status with the secret knowledge that she is most likely, in fact, unfulfilled. An ambitious "career woman" whose femininity is constantly challenged can begin to internalize those doubts and thus undermine her success, just as a working "supermom," fearful that one really can't have it all, may engineer her own unhappiness (Applegarth, 1976; Person, 1982; Kanefield, 1985; Moulton, 1986). Lesbians, ever invisible, have been absent from the debates on female generativity—just as the notion of a lesbian mother has been, until quite recently, largely an oxymoron.

Freud's psychosexual theory echoed the late Victorian cultural prescription for women to forsake their subjective sexual selves, their sense of agency, in pursuit of their seemingly illusive femininity (Harris, 1991). The quintessential actualization of that femininity was represented culturally in the role of wife and mother.

Resistance to these prescribed roles—in the form of alternative sexual preference or the maintenance of desires whose actualization lie outside the domestic arena—have resulted in pathologizing explanations usually having to do with some form of unresolved "masculinity complex" (Horney, 1926) and its ubiquitous progenitor, penis envy (Freud, 1925). Thus, for decades in this country career women (often a code for the invisible lesbian) have been maligned as "not real women"—that is, assumed to have some form of internalized male identification (Person, 1982; Kanter, 1977; Kanefield, 1985; Moulton, 1986). Career ambition and motherhood seemed to be at odds in those social classes where work was not an economic necessity.

Lesbians (as well as heterosexual women who choose to be child free) are often caught between the generative matrices of what McAdams & St. Aubin (1992) have called "cultural demand" and "inner desire." How is one to deconstruct what may appear phenomenologically as an "inner desire" to be generative in ways other than by mothering, when the "cultural demand" is to affirm one's femininity through the maternal/heterosexual connection?

Ireland (1993) attempts to address this conflation of motherhood and female identity. She suggests that child-free women can serve as a third term in the Lacanian sense and disrupt the path to normative female identity that traditionally includes reproduction. "By indicating the reality that women can be other than mothers, these women created a 'space' between the daughter and her mother's identity—a space in which alternative female identities might be imagined" (p. 118.).

Child-free women act as a third term in their status as "undecidable"—that is, a term that cannot be assimilated within the traditional binaries of male or female (Ireland, 1993, p. 132). The destabilization of traditional gender categories, of course, is what being a lesbian is all about. Ireland's analysis of the patriarchal attempt to render the child-free woman "invisible" speaks to a common lesbian experience as well:

> Women who are not mothers threaten society with a loss of the presumed adult identity for women. By not ever becoming mothers and invalidating by their very presence the universality of this restricted female identity, they may also seem to undermine the bases of gender identity for men. This subtle, and perhaps deeper threat, helps explain why patriarchal society seems to have a stake in keeping the childless woman as the 'invisible woman,' particularly when she elects her childless state with scant signs of anguish or deviance. Men who strongly identify with being the opposite of women-mothers will find these new women destabilizing. Women whose identities are also firmly attached to the woman-mother identity need sameness rather

than similarity in their relationship with women and will also have
trouble finding a way to connect meaningfully with the childless
woman. (pp. 133–134)

What is problematic in Ireland's work is her insistence that the path
to a satisfactory adult female identity for the woman who is not a
mother must include an encounter with her lack of having/desiring a
child. From there, she enters a Winnicottian-like potential space from
which she can create or be generative in alternative ways. And although
Ireland allows for different paths to that apparently universal
encounter, she suggests quite plainly that the state of being child
free/childless entails an absence for women that must be reckoned with.

Generativity, then, entails a shift from a space of emptiness (the lack
of desire for a child, the lack of the means or opportunity to bear a
child) to a potential space of creativity. "But with the universal social
expectation that women should be mothers, regardless of their own
personal experience of the 'absence,' the idea of absence is always present in their shift as an emptiness, rather than as a generative space.
When there is a shift to childlessness as a generative space the childless
woman is on the threshold of expanding her experience of female subjectivity" (Ireland, 1993, p. 125).

Ireland does not revert to a strict biodeterminism, though she may as
well have, as the reader senses the inexorable pull toward universals in
her theory of social construction. Heterosexuality is largely assumed in
Ireland's work. Lesbians are given token inclusion, but not separate
consideration. The transformative woman, in Ireland's categories, is the
woman who finds her wish to bear a child lacking. She is the trailblazer.
"She is more likely to have organized her identity around autonomy;
because of this she can be judged by others as having a 'masculinity
complex.' . . . It is not surprising that these women tend to remain
'invisible' in discussions of adult development because their presence
challenges many unconsciously accepted preconceptions of what

women 'should be'" (Ireland, 1993, p. 70). These sentences could very easily have been written about lesbians in our culture; Ireland acknowledges that many but certainly not all lesbians fall into this category.

There is the notion that a woman must confront her lack of the wish for a child before she is able to move into a transitional creative space. Ultimately, this privileges a woman's biological reproductive capacities in a manner that has not been manifest in clinical work with lesbians. Even for Ireland, it appears to be destabilizing to consider the possibility that for many women their reproductive capacity is but one of many potentials that they may or may not utilize.

For lesbians, the struggle has more often been to claim psychologically their right to mother, as the cultural construction of lesbians as "not real women" has been internalized and incorporated into lesbian identities. For lesbians, the issue has not been one of desire, but rather finding the opportunity to be truly generative in alternative milieus (as educators, mentors in the business world, artists, community leaders) without having to be other than who they are.

Although Ireland never deals with construct of generativity per se, and is very clear to articulate the impact of culture on the reproduction of mothering, there is a ghost of classical theory haunting her work. The implication for this reader is that generativity is, in essence, a sublimation of maternal energy. That implication persists because Ireland has not questioned the assumption of a gendered self that is based on unitary same-sexed identifications. She only begins to approach a critique when she suggests that girls may form part identifications with other aspects of Mother that do not have to do with maternal function.

Once we begin to think not of the development of a unified female identity but rather of gendered subjectivities, we create the space for the psychoanalytical understanding of a history of internalized interactions. It is a history that allows for cross-gender, transgendered, and same-sex identifications within a complex nonlinear matrix of gendered selves a history of internalized interaction and identification that provide the basis for a generativity that stands outside the reproductive arena.

## generativity as motherhood

Generativity has been linked for so long to a heterosexually based gender identity that it has been difficult to think of it outside the confines of that biological bases of reproduction. Erik Erikson introduced the continuum of "Generativity versus Stagnation" as a stage in the life cycle, the seventh of eight stages of development. Generativity was defined as occurring when "a meeting of bodies and minds leads to a gradual expansion of ego interest and to a libidinal involvement in that which is generated. Failure to do so leads to an obsessive need for pseudo-intimacy with a pervading sense of stagnation and personal impoverishment" (Erikson, 1950, p. 267).

Erikson's theory of the life cycle is embedded in his commitment to the concept of epigenesis, a biologically based construct of species development that is borrowed from the field of embryology. It is, in essence, a critical stage theory. Thus Erikson outlines a developmental progression that may vary in content from culture to culture depending on its *ethosa* (1985), but it is a progression whose stages—coupled as they are with Freud's theory of psychosexual developments—suggest universal heterosexuality.

Erikson's early work reified Freud's essentialist presentation of masculine and feminine modes as active and passive, respectively—a gender binary that Erikson saw represented in children's play. With the reification of the phallic intrusive mode for little boys and the passive inclusive mode for little girls (the emblem of which was his teleological explanation of why it was that little boys built towers with their blocks in the nursery, while little girls played house and filled "empty spaces"), the feminist community understandably has largely ignored Erikson's work.

In an unspecified but clear response to the feminist critique, Erikson (1985) modified his rigid adherence to the gender bifurcation of classical psychosexual theory, allowing for greater personal and cultural variation. With a reluctant nod to a constitutionally based bisexuality, he considers the possibility of a more active subjective femininity, noting that "the 'inner space' . . . is by no means at odds with a full expression of vigorous intrusiveness in locomotion and in general patterns of initiative" (p. 37). However, he warns us, this bisexual disposition (greater liability of intrusive and inclusive modes) does not foreclose an implicitly normative heterosexuality.

Erikson follows Benedek (1973), who suggests that we have an instinctual drive toward procreation, the sublimation of which allows for the possibility of an energic shift, the use of libidinal forces in psychosocial contexts for "productivity and creativity in the service of the generations" (Benedek, 1973, p. 53)

In its earliest conception, (Erikson, 1950), generativity was clearly linked with procreation, and generativity was assumed to beget parenting. Throughout his work, Erikson remains grounded in the biodeterminist drive/conflict model. Moreover, Erikson has been critiqued for his rigid adherence to hierarchical sequences of development (Seligman, & Shanok, 1995). But subsequent life-span theorists and researchers (Levinson, 1978; Gilligan, 1982; Baruch, Barnett, & Rivers, 1983; Ryff, & Heincke, 1983; McAdams, Ruetzel & Foley 1986; A. Schwartz, 1994) have seized upon the concept of generativity as touching something vital in the adult experience and have stripped it of its conceptual linkage to the biological.

Kotre (1984) identifies four different forms of generativity, each of which he sees as a way to transcend oneself in time:

- Biological generativity is the sheer production of offspring, the passing on of genetic material through genes.
- Parental generativity is the nurturing of children (not necessarily one's own).
- Technical generativity is teaching—that is, the passing on of knowledge, skills, and expertise.

- Cultural generativity consists of multiform contributions to society that may take place in the world of ideas and ideology, art, business, and, though not specifically stated, political action.

Generativity is one constitutive of an everchanging narrative of identity through which an individual provides her life with unity, purpose, and meaning (McAdams & St. Aubin, 1992). McAdams (1985) categorizes generativity themes along parameters of power and intimacy. Power narratives emphasize generativity through an expansion of self, which impacts on the environment through the exertion of force or control. Intimacy narratives emphasize generativity through the cultivation of interpersonal relationships embodying care and concern. McAdams & St. Aubin (1992) recognize, however, that the implementation of these narratives in the world requires societal opportunities—certainly an external if not internal barrier for lesbians. It is important to bear in mind that psychoanalytic studies of the developmental issues of adulthood are scarce (Alonso & Schippers, 1986), and that those concentrating primarily on lesbian development do not even touch on the concept of generativity (Eisenbud, 1982; Abelove, et. al, 1993; Magee & Miller, 1992; O'Connor & Ryan, 1993; Glassgold & Iasenza, 1995).

Although the heterosexist bias endemic to Erikson is clear, he has named a phenomenon that has become more and more salient in the consulting room. Child-free lesbians often express a deep sense of loss or projected impoverishment if they foresee a life that is foreclosed from the possibilities of transcending more immediate narcissistic interests through generative participation in the broader culture.[1] Often implicit here is the misunderstanding, often not consciously stated, that generativity is not exclusively related to parenting. They know, but do not *know*, that one may parent and not feel generative. It is the unwitting foreclosure of parenting, mentoring, or other forms of participation in transgenerational community life that may be a serious bar to the actualization of generative needs. How does this come about?

For many lesbians, internalized homophobia can act as a bar to generativity (Margolies, Becker, & Jackson-Brewer, 1987). The denigration and/or repression of desire has a direct effect on the agentic functions of one who produces or creates. Moreover, what is there to "pass on," within a generational context, if what one *is* feels contaminated, tainted by the culturally constructed abjectness of the lesbian self?

### clinical anecdote

Brenda had been a promising, somewhat idiosyncratic, playwright early in her career, but her last play, written shortly before she entered analysis and specifically written to reach a wider mainstream audience, had failed. Brenda entered analysis severely depressed, "blocked" in her work, and in an unsatisfactory relation of stasis with a lover of many years with whom she did not live.

Born into an affluent WASP family in the Midwest, Brenda was sent to a prestigious girls' boarding school to complete her secondary education. During her final year, Brenda had a mild "breakdown" that coincided with both her parents' impending divorce and a homosexual "panic." Through a haze of alcohol (the family currency), Brenda realized that she was a lesbian, and she went home to "come out." Her family, siblings included, were shocked and rejecting. Disconsolate, Brenda, returned to school to finish the term, graduate, and effect a pseudo-separation from her family, at which time she dove into the more inclusive literary/art world and seemingly eschewed the traditional conservative value system of her family. It soon became clear in the analysis that most of Brenda's professional achievements were geared toward gaining the love and respect of her narcissistic mother, who acknowledged but did not *recognize* Brenda as a separate person.[2]

Brenda's love for her mother was intense, and the distance at which her mother held her was interpreted by Brenda as a profound rejection of her self and her sexuality.[3] Moreover, Brenda's mother would brook no competition from rival objects; she virtually denied her daughter's lover, whom she saw as both a threat to her bottomless claims for attention and as a testimony to her daughter's own sexual powers and desirability.

Brenda's despair at achieving more widespread acclaim and appreciation reflected her despair at her invisibility in the face of her narcissistic mother, who claimed hegemony over sexuality in all forms. (Hence Brenda's transferential conviction, early on in the analysis, that real success would mark the end of her relationship with her lover and, of course, with the analyst as well.) Although her writing had seemed to arise as a refuge from and means of dealing with the turmoil at home, slowly and painfully Brenda began to see the ways in which her work was inextricably bound to those early internal objects. Moreover, it was difficult for Brenda to acknowledge her own shame and self-denigration of her sexuality. After all, she was an "out" professional, strongly identified as feminist; the prodigal in the family whose overt rebellion masked an inner desperation for recognition and approval.

As Brenda began a new performance piece and tried it out in workshop, she found a very receptive lesbian audience. But this engendered torturous conflicts about being identified as a "lesbian playwright," about not wanting to be ghettoized, about wanting to reach a wider audience. But who was Brenda's audience: the "downtown" literati, her community of colleagues and friends, or the conservative, mainstream, "family" of her roots? Sexual inhibitions, ensued and Brenda seemed devoid of a once-searing passion both for her lover and other women.

Brenda was no longer comfortable with the scenarios of dominance and submission that had often brought her to orgasm. Fantasies of sexual submission, once exciting, seemed now to be a reflection of the abjectness of her lesbian self. The analysis was long and arduous. She became less and less able to write anything at all. Brenda traversed periods of great despair as she struggled in vain for a relationship with her mother that felt real and faced the terror of the apparent vanishing of her creativity.

At the approach of one planned holiday visit to her mother, Brenda impulsively called to cancel, a rare event for the dutiful daughter. "I realized that if I went to see her I'd have to kill myself." And although Brenda was terrified at feeling on the cusp of suicide, what was clear was that couldn't yet visit and retain her self. She could no longer bear functioning as a part-object.

In the middle phase of the analysis, Brenda wrote what she considered to be her best play. It was in a "different voice" and dealt with her life in the gay and lesbian metropolis in which she lived. The production of this play coincided with Brenda's cohabitation with her lover and the insistent introduction of this lover as a permanent "family member" to her parents and siblings.

There were other generative changes as well. Brenda began a literary journal with a community of friends. Her relationship with her students slowly changed, becoming at once more boundaried and less rigid, noticeably infused with a creativity that Brenda feared she had lost. In addition, Brenda helped to found an alternative theater workshop where plays of lesbian and gay themes (though not exclusively so) could be produced. Incredibly active, productive, and generative, in every sense of the word, Brenda had broken through the depression, the ennui, the threat of the enveloping nothingness, largely as a result of her being more at ease with her sexuality and working through of her relationship with her internal objects.

During this time, a niece was born with whom Brenda developed a close relationship. She wished to pass on her world: the world of art, literature, and the theater, a different world from her family of origin. Brenda initially was very identified with this niece and wanted both to protect and to offer her relational options that she was denied as a child: to be recognized in her subjectivity rather than as a part-object for narcissistic caregivers.

Throughout Brenda's analysis, the recurrent theme was one of recognition and agency, which manifested in her attempts to reclaim herself as a writer. Over and over, Brenda was shocked to discover how inextricably her writerly self was linked with her desire—its acknowledgment and expression. More obvious to her were issues of separation from her mother and consequent boundary conflicts with her lover, dystonic identifications with a depressed schizoid father, and problems with her own affect regulation.

Alonso & Schippers (1986), among the few writers who have attempted to integrate object relations theory with the development of generativity, suggest that true generativity requires the attainment of the depressive position (Klein, 1948). The goal of the depressive position is integration:

> Split off parts of the historical self are able to be united into a more complete self, the "good-enough self." Internal object representations which have historically been distorted through the defensive operation of splitting and projective identification are able to be clarified in the "good enough object world" and a new level of awareness about the self and the world. (Alonso & Schippers, 1986, p. 9)

Self-psychology, too, speaks to the necessity of a good-enough object world. In his last paper, Kohut (1982) wrote of a concept related to generativity, which he termed intergenerational continuity, and involves a joyful affirmation of the younger generation's right to unfold—which in turn requires an internalization of a "good" self-object (p. 402). Hence, bars to that "good enough self" become bars to generative extension.

The integrations of which Alonso speaks also include socially constructed gender splits: the arbitrary binaries of activity/passivity, autonomy/dependence, masculine/feminine, heterosexual/homosexual—which form the cognitive organizers of our world (Kohlberg, 1966; Dimen, 1991). For lesbians, gay men, and women who choose to remain child free, it can be particularly difficult to maintain an ongoing experience of a "good-enough self," of one who has something of value to pass on. And representations of selves that are damaged or mutant (as is common with internalized homophobia), conflations of sexuality with other "bad-me" internalizations, misattunements and inadequate mirroring—all create barriers to generative extension (Mahler, Pine, & Bergman, 1975; Stern, 1985; A. Schwartz, 1986).

By extension, I am referring to the passing on to others what one has learned—not simply concrete knowledge, but also the wisdom and the articulation of values that are embedded in the idiosyncrasies of particular historical experience and more general ways of being in the world (A. Schwartz, 1994). Generativity for lesbians (defined for these purposes as a claimed identity or partial-identity amid other identities of gender, race, class, religion, ethnicity, and so forth) may include parenting in various forms: as a biological or adoptive mother, as a coparent in a nuclear or extended collective family. Generative extension may involve teaching or some sort of mentoring.[4] For women and men, however, regardless of their parenting status, generative extension involves participation in a political, cultural, or creative community in a way that passes on within an individuated intersubjective context.

Generativity is also a relation of care. In Eriksonian terms, that means "a widening commitment to take care of the persons, the products, and the ideas one has learned to care for" (Erikson 1985, p. 67). Clinically, one may think of a continuum from a narcissistically based self-encapsulation through a capacity for concern and care for psychically differentiated others (Winnicott, 1963).

Generativity, defined here as a process of generative extension through relations of care, may also facilitate the reconfiguring of internal object world, just as a transactional spiral of interaction with one's children may facilitate a reworking of early developmental stages, allowing for real intrapsychic change (Benedek, 1973; A. Schwartz, 1994). However, the capacity for concern rests not only on a history of successful integration of split objects but also on an object world that allows for successful reparation. Thus, a caregiver/family/society that rejects an individual's repeated efforts to contribute will find itself in danger of discovering that capacity for concern eroded. A lesbian—often barred from asserting herself for fear of disclosure—faces the danger that external conditions will resonate all too closely with early intrapsychic ones. Internalized homophobia often erodes a lesbian's sense that she has something of value to pass on.

The actualization of generative needs requires the experiencing of subjectivity, an empowered sense of agency that is capable of empathic, reflective giving to an Other (singular or collective) whose subjectivity is equally recognized and respected. The analytic task, within a clinical context, is the identification and working through of obstacles to a woman's/lesbian's achievement of full generativity. Internalized gender/sexual identities that are constricted or conflictual can be central in paralyzing the generative self. The analysis is facilitated by looking to confusions, crucial internalizations and consolidations of identity that occurred during key periods of development: early caretaking dyads, periods of separation, triangulation, and adolescence. The availability of the analyst to serve as a transferential object of both romantic and identificatory love is vital in establshing that subjective sense of self.

## generativity and gender

Benedicte was a young writer, a lesbian, who sought out French psychoanalyst Joyce McDougall for consultation to help her understand and work through a crippling writer's block (McDougall, 1991). McDougall tells us that after two years of psychoanalysis, the writer's block appeared to be resolved—a function, McDougall presumed, of Benedicte's emotional reconnection with a father who had died when she was fifteen months of age. According to McDougall, "Both her homosexuality and her writing career were paths of identifications with him" (p. 560). In the sixth year of treatment, shortly before both analyst and analysand were seriously considering termination, Benedicte was forced to undergo a hysterectomy due to severe endometriosis. The hysterectomy seemed to precipitate a reappearance of the troublesome writer's block.

During the course of this phase of the analysis, Benedicte brought in evidence of an unconscious fantasy, which suggested to McDougall that Benedicte felt her mother was somehow responsible for the hysterectomy. "In her associations it becomes clear that this aspect of the internalized mother has attacked her sexuality and destroyed her capacity to bear children" (p. 561). Although McDougall treated this fantasy as a projection of Benedicte's own fantasized "crime" of killing her father and destroying her mother's chance to have more babies, Benedicte's own words suggested another strand of interpretation: "The truth is I didn't believe I could become pregnant because I'm not real in that way" (p. 563). "Martians don't have babies," McDougall responded. The Martian metaphor had been introduced by McDougall a few years earlier in the treatment, in response to Benedicte's claim that she was neither male nor female. McDougall missed out here on a rather common complaint of lesbians heard in the consulting room—that they aren't *real girls*, which most often means they have neither internalized a heterosexually defined femininity/womanhood nor chosen or been permitted a fundamental identification with their maternal caretaker.

In this case, Benedicte was deprived of a basic identification with a non-narcissistic, growth-fostering, loving, maternal, female object. It was not the "Penis-legs" that Benedicte was missing (a reference to a dream that they had worked on) but rather a functioning maternal representation with whom Benedicte could identify. Perhaps Benedicte's fantasy of her mother's attacks on her (pro)creativity were not merely projections of fantasized retaliations but in essence accurate reflections of a jealous and competitive mother seeking to exclude her daughter from the heterosexual arena.[5]

Consider Benedicte's memory that as a young girl, she had been given twin dolls, one a boy and the other a girl, as a birthday gift.

Benedicte preferred the boy doll and played almost exclusively with him. With apparent consternation, one day Benedict's mother declared that the dolls had to go to the doll hospital. When the dolls returned, they were both girls.

An alternative constructive of Benedicte's internal world might suggest that one aspect of Benedict's maternal object came in the guise of her *father* who had cared for her as an infant. Her longing was for the maternal father, not the phallic father of separation and difference.

McDougall concludes that Benedicte's "literary characters would only acquire the space to live *their* lives when *she*, their creator, appropriated her father's voice, the 'presence and force' of a man's difference. The course of the analysis, as noted at the outset, would show Benedicte's writing career and homosexuality to be different paths of identification with this long-lost much-beloved father" (p. 581). It is McDougall's adherence to the rigid sex/gender binaries that precludes her from seeing the father as being a maternal, generative figure as well.

McDougall grants us all our bisexuality (1991), but it is a sexuality grounded in the "bi-nary" of mimetic sex/gender relations. As a homosexual women, it is taken for granted that Benedicte will have a primary male identification. And it is this fictive male identification, according to McDougall, that gives life to her fiction!

But there is no evidence that Benedicte was primarily "male identified." She was not female like her mother and hence did not fit into traditional gender binaries; that sense of not fitting, of being an alien, is a common complaint of lesbians who have rejected certain aspects of their maternal identifications and fear that they have nothing to put in their place. I would argue that Benedicte was struggling to find a place for her femaleness, nurtured as it was, in a soil of multigendered maternal and paternal representations. It is in this way that she found her unique path to generativity.

Earlier in the chapter, we saw that Brenda's generativity was inhibited by her internalized homophobia. The theme there was that her creative agency was a function of an intersubjective recognition of a lesbian self, which allowed for the flowering of generative expression. Does this identification of a "lesbian self" include, preclude, or exclude an identification with a female self, a maternal self, a parental self. Is there a way in which gender and gender-role identity interweave with reproductive generativity, and is that interweaving of a sociocultural or intrapsycich fabric?

Issues of *reproduction*, whether to have a family and how, can have special meaning for lesbians. With the rejection of heterosexuality comes a sometimes intentional and at other times unintended excision of maternal identity as incompatible with a lesbian identity (Weston, 1991). This excision may resonate deeply with the culture's identification of lesbians as women whose "femininity"—whose very womanliness—is in question (Magee & Miller, 1992).

In Freud's (1920) "Psychogenesis of a Case of Female Homosexuality," he ascribes the emergence of the young girl's homoerotic interest to some amalgam of oedipal disappointments, a strong "masculinity complex" from childhood (read penis envy), and constitutional masculine proclivities.[6] Moreover, he counterpoises the "maternal attitude" with homosexual desire as he traces the onset of his young patient's homosexuality to the birth of a younger brother in the midst of her adolescence. At sixteen, according to Freud, Mother's successful oedipal victory (as evidenced by the birth of a sibling) turned the teenager away from men altogether in revenge against the father and ultimately all men. When mother birthed a rival brother, Freud surmises that the girl's nascent "maternal attitude" was turned in, so to speak, for the homoerotic pursuit of a mature women.

### clinical anecdote

A young lesbian's lover became pregnant on her third attempt at alternative intrauterine insemination. Upon telling her office mates about it, a new heterosexual father respond with a joke about how difficult the ensuing nine months can be for "us guys."

Hurt and angry at the obvious implications, Suzanne looked forward to telling a gay male colleague and friend the news. To her amazement, they too refered to her as a "father or whatever you are." Suzanne did not feel ready for pregnancy herself—largely as a function of the scars of an abusive childhood that she was working through in analysis, but also because of her persistent feelings that she was "not a real girl."

It was not until a popular film emerged in which a man becomes pregnant and delivers a baby that Suzanne joked with a note of bitter-sweet irony that maybe biological motherhood could be an option for her as well as for her lover. "If Arnold Schwartzenegger can have a baby, than maybe I can too." She too confused her feeling of not being a "real girl" like her heterosexual counterparts with being male. It is a cultural conflation that has inflicted many wounds and caused many analyses to go awry (Blechner, 1993).

In earlier work (A. Schwartz, 1984b, 1986, 1988b, 1994), I have attempted to describe a certain form of internalized gender-role iden-tity that I have termed *not female like Mother* or *de-identification with Mother as female*, which some lesbians begin to assume during the period of triangulation partly in response to an increasing awareness of gender privilege and the positioning of subjectivity that are manifest in their parental dynamics. The consequences of such an internalization may be significant for lesbians who wish to mother or become part of a family in which they will raise children.[7]

It might seem theoretically contradictory to speak on the one hand of a multiplicity of genders and their representations in the construc-tion of lesbian identities, as has been the current of this work; and then to offer the notion of a refused identification or disidentification as a bar to lesbians who wish to mother. There is a tension, but not quite a paradox. The process of internalization is intrinsic to, but not synony-mous with, identification. Moreover, the idea of multiple fluid and complementary identities in no way discounts such internal processes (Benjamin, 1995).

Having an identification that might be articulated as not female like Mother, can and most often does exist among other internalized identifications. However, de-identification with Mother as female often renders one at odds with mothering as our culture constructs it. Clinically, it becomes necessary to understand the historical bases of these refused identifications, which tend to erode the sense of maternal adequacy and agency that accompanies full generativity in this arena.

## reproductive crises

It might be interesting, at this point, to compare two analytic cases where there were difficulties with conception to see how they how they varied with respect to issues of gender. The first, Gabrielle, is heterosexually identified; the second, Jane, identifies as a lesbian. In no way are these clinical vignettes posited as representative of their respective categories, but rather they are offered to illustrate the additional weight that internalized questions of gender might come to bear on lesbians attempting to form families with children.

## gabrielle

Gabrielle was twenty-four, a bright but somewhat obsessive-compulsive young woman, quite isolated from her feelings, married to a man more than twice her age. It was a good match in most respects, providing the continued "parenting" she still needed with the respectful support of an attentive lover. Despite the fact that Lawrence was in his fifties and had already raised two boys, Gabrielle very much wanted a baby. She was a plagued by a sense of restlessness, a lack of being able to settle into something, a sense that she was "wandering around."

Gabrielle's parents presented somewhat of an enigma. She had "shut down" with them in pre-adolescence, and they shared virtually none of their inner lives. Mother loomed largest as a figure of betrayal; during

Gabrielle's childhood, she would periodically lapse into seemingly unpredictable rages—often over music lessons (Mother was arthritic and suffered great problems with her own mobility and dexterity)—and hit Gabrielle. To make matters worse, Gabrielle could not predict when her mother might become angry and when she might surprise with understanding. Father took a back seat in childrearing, and Gabrielle seemed to have nothing but the most perfunctory relationship with him. Gabrielle reported a relentless work ethic in the household; the parents busied themselves with various domestic projects and expected the children to do likewise unless they were otherwise occupied outside of the house. Daydreaming, idle reading, were frowned upon.

As an adolescent Gabrielle, managed her anger, frustrations, and anxieties by compulsively making and executing endless lists of tasks. She stayed away from the house as much as possible, engaging in a variety of athletic activities. She left home as soon as possible and now visits perhaps once a year. Gabrielle would not think of telling her mother about her wishes or trials in attempting to become pregnant.

Work in art history did not quite satisfy. There were obvious narcissistic issues connected to her feelings of being unappreciated and illtreated, but they were rarely engageable in the therapeutic work. Gabrielle began a Master's program, but it too was largely in the service of structuring her day, another series of activities meant to oblate feelings or the lack thereof.

After the first year of graduate work, Gabrielle and her husband tried to become pregnant in earnest. Their efforts failed and a fertility workup indicated that Lawrence's sperm count was somewhat low and the sperm irregularly shaped; but it was primarily the blockages in Gabrielle's fallopian tubes and an allegedly "hostile" vaginal environment that accounted for their difficulties in conceiving. First they "charted" assiduously to time their attempts more exactly to Gabrielle's ovulatory periods. Then Gabrielle had laproscopic surgery, followed by monthly inseminations performed by a fertility specialist.

Throughout this period Gabrielle became increasingly depressed. She hated the repeated violations to her body and despaired at the apparent "fact" that there was something very wrong with her. Obviously she was barren, defective in some way, "couldn't produce anything." At no time during this period, however, did she talk about her womanhood or make reference to her femininity. The injury seemed gender free and revolved around a narcissistic sense of herself as capable of perfection. Her body was betraying her and she felt punished for some unknown and unknowable wrong, a repetition of her mother's attacks on her and her failure to produce perfectly.

### jane

Jane is a forty-year-old professional woman, living in a long-term relationship with her lesbian lover. Jane's pride in being a lesbian and her overt rejection of stereotypic heterosexual gender roles belied her fundamental sense of an inadequate and marred internal representation of a gendered self. Although Jane claimed to want a family, she had long eschewed motherhood on the assumption that she was "not a real girl." Difficulties in negotiating rapprochement with a depressed and overwhelmed mother, who was envious of her child's youthful sense of energy and *joie de vivre*, coupled with a rather aloof father who had difficulty being intimate with women, facilitated an early de-identification with mother-as-female (A. Schwartz, 1984b). Jane's father rejected her persistent efforts to be like him—refusing, for example, to teach her the carpentry that was the love of his life. She couldn't be his "son," and she didn't want to be her mother's daughter.

For the analyst-father, the patient wanted to be perfect in the hopes of finally being special—but then resented wanting that from an endemically unresponsive, disappointing source. It was this paternal imago for whom she was working professionally, and thus it became clear why work became such a difficult, ungratifying, and ultimately lonely experience. However, most of the transference fell within the purview of the maternal. The analyst soon became the critical, envious, and occasionally humiliating mother, who didn't want the patient to be a "real girl." Moreover, "real girls" were not so enticing because, in the patient's view, they were frustrated, unactualized, depressed people who seethed with the resentment of having missed out on life.

As these fragmented parts of her gender apperceptions were examined within the analysis, Jane became aware of a deep and profound wish to bear a child. She began a series of alternative inseminations that forced her to confront her characterological passivity, pseudocompliance with authority, and her fear of oedipal competition with a mother who was it, seemed, truly envious and exclusionary (McDougall, 1980; Eisenbud, 1982).

For Jane, coming to the decision to parent facilitated the first steps toward the actualization of her generative needs. Up until this time, with the exception of her sexual preference, Jane had been a chronically perfectionistic "good child" who performed in the hope of being recognized by the professional "daddies" in her life, not for her femininity but for her achievements. For Jane, the decision to mother was an embrace of one aspect of a longed-for maternal identification.

In her pursuit of alternative insemination, she needed to "come out" to various authorities and thus identify herself in some way as a sexual outlaw. When fertility became a question, she sought out appropriate expertise with alacrity. She also began a support group of other prospective lesbian parenting couples. Each of these activities was extremely uncharacteristic of her former, rather isolated, passive, child self. Jane was a professional who had failed *three times* to finish the specialization program in her field. She was now able to finish and assumed a position of leadership with it.

As the fates would have it, Jane learned that she was not able to conceive. Painful as that was, Jane is now prepared to make an active choice about having children in her life. Her lover might birth a child, they might adopt, Jane might choose to relate to children in her life in a different way or, ultimately, not at all. The critical point here is that Jane's analysis allowed a reworking of an early gender identification so that she was able to think about her generative needs from a sense of a subjective generative self.

## lesbians are mothers

As there has been a growing foundation for women loving women within the culture, and as women have increasingly availed themselves of advances in reproductive technology, a quiet revolution has been brewing. As the discourse grows, the revolution grows louder and more articulate.

Lesbians are having children. They are birthing them, adopting them, coparenting them.[8] Lesbians are creating families and, as they do, traditional heterosexual, homosexual, and mental health communities are turning upside down.

One lesbian couple with a child in the making, seeks out surrogate grandparents as substitutes for the nonaccepting grandparents in the family. Another has a "naming" ceremony for a six-month-old child born through alternative fertilization to one member of a lesbian couple who is partnered to a divorced mother of an eleven-year-old boy in a new lesbian-step family; here, both sets of grandparents attend the ceremony as well as friends of the family. Poems, songs, and stories are offered in honor of the baby by participating guests.

Informal, community-based support groups for lesbian mothers are proliferating. Serving as arenas for discussion of traditional child rearing issues, they also form a network of support for interfacing with heterosexually dominated institutions. The groups obviously vary in content and structure depending on the needs of the participants. Whereas one group might restrict its membership exclusively to "out" lesbian mothers, another sees itself as a group for alternative families and consists of two lesbian couples and their children and two single moms, one heterosexual and the other bisexually identified. The children of the group have been adopted domestically and from abroad or conceived through alternative fertilization. One of the sperm donors is known and acknowledged, though largely nonparticipatory; the other two are unknown. Come the holidays, these children and their families celebrate together as well as with their individual families of origin.

## the lesbian generation gap

This postmodern "post-feminist" age has spawned a fairly noticeable lesbian generation gap in which young women do not appear to have the same conflicts and coparenting with the confluence of motherhood and sexuality as do their elder sisters. Many assume that they will raise children and live in families—why not? Raised on an MTV world of androgyny and pan-sexuality, being a lesbian is "no big deal." Although the social stresses and real discriminations attendant to being a lesbian cannot be easily dismissed, it has been my clinical experience that these young women are at a much greater level of intrapsychic comfort than the age cohort who "came out" in the 1960s, 1970s, or before.

Similarly, the first generation of out lesbian mothers (those whose children were conceived within heterosexual couplings that later dissolved) had a very different set of experiences from second-generation lesbian mothers who conceived of their families as lesbians and are raising them in that context. First-generation lesbians, when divorcing a man to be with another woman, had to contend more frontally with the integration of their sexuality with motherhood. A woman's active sexuality is "in your face" in a way it never need be in a heterosexual union, confronting and contradicting the culture's presumption of lesbian mother as oxymoron. Second-generation lesbians do not seem to feel the injunction proffered by Freud (1920) of trading in their "maternal attitude" for desire.

Moreover, there is a new discourse on families. Lesbians and gay men question not so much the "naturalness" of a biological tie, but rather the assumption that shared biogenetic substance in itself confers kinship (Weston, 1991). In what Weston has termed the re-engineering of biogenetics, the open existence of gay and lesbian families displaces biogenetic symbolism of kinship as hegemonic and replaces it with communities of choice. Chosen families do not necessarily entail rejection from or rejection of traditional biological families; they are an addition to most lesbians' lives.

We might think of lesbian families, chosen families, as a kind of third term in a family discourse that functions outside the realm of biogenetically determined kinship. Such a third term might obviate the political disavowal/psychic negation of the biogenetic family, which has become a feature of certain segments of the gay community (Altman, 1979).

The lesbian generation gap is apparent with the academic arena as well. For the researcher, the zeitgeist has changed profoundly over the past twenty years. Ellen Lewin (1993) writes of the circumstances surrounding the birthing of her groundbreaking research on lesbian mothers, which she conducted from 1977 to 1981. She notes that, in the mid-seventies when she was doing her preliminary research, there were very few scholarly works written about lesbian mothers. Most of the literature was about custody cases, whereby the state or their familial representatives challenged a lesbian's right to custody of her child or children. Lewin had to consider how to frame her socio/psychological interest in lesbian mothers in order to get funding for the project. All advisers recommended that she keep the "L" word in low profile (make no mention of it in the title of the grant proposal) and that she should frame the research within the context of single motherhood. It wasn't until more than a decade later, with the growth of lesbian and gay studies, that Lewin felt able to "out" her own research project in a way that would not jeopardize her legitimacy in the academic world (p. xvi).

The original research compares lesbian mothers and single (aka heterosexual) mothers. It is emblematic of a societal stance that maintains the incompatibility of motherhood and sexuality that, within the sample, one-half of the lesbians and one-third of the heterosexual mothers had coresident partners (Lewin & Lyons, 1982). Yet they qualified as single.

Lewin wanted to demonstrate that lesbian mothers were as good as other mothers, just as much of psychological, feminist-informed research in the 1980s sought to demonstrate that there was no psychopathology endemic to children of lesbian mothers (Kirkpatrick, Smith, & Roy, 1981). Lewin found what she was looking for. In the sample, the women's identities as mothers seemed to subsume their identities as lesbians and to erase most differences between the heterosexual and lesbian "single mothers." How could it be otherwise since, as Lewin admits, the research erased the sexuality of both?

A decade later, Lewin (1993) acknowledges that her findings were consonant with her expectations. She realizes that the narrative generated by her structured interviewing was born of the cultural matrix in which they were embedded, a matrix that erases the sexuality of both groups. However, Lewin points to an interesting paradox contained within the identity of a lesbian mother:

> Insofar as lesbianism and motherhood seem to be culturally (if not biologically) incompatible, they transcend or challenge the ordinary organization of gender in American culture, which conflates "woman" and "mother" and defines lesbians as neither. In this sense, claiming the identity of lesbian mother may be construed as an instance of *resistance* to prevailing sexual politics.
>
> But in becoming mothers, lesbians join heterosexual women in a particular organization of identity which partakes of mainstream gender ideology. . . . This suggests that the resistance to conventional gender ideology implied by the oxymoronic status of the lesbian mother can be suspended or compromised by its resolution of the "problem of lesbian identity." Though I do not argue that lesbians become mothers purposefully in order to regularize their status, as a direct response to

stigma, I do contend that motherhood directly enables women (whether lesbian or heterosexual) to claim a specific location in the gender system. (pp. 15–16; italics mine)

The postmodern critique has allowed us to understand that any one identity, be it lesbian, mother, or lesbian mother, is but a fetter in a fool's chain of one's own making. Still, recalling the chant of lesbian mothers marching in protest in 1994—"We're here, we're gay, we're in the PTA"—reminds us that assuming a recognizable identity of lesbian mother remains both an internal and external hurdle for many.[9]

For lesbians wishing to raise children, there are many issues that present themselves for consideration. How is the child to be acquired, through birthing or by adoption?[10] If biologically, then how is that child to be conceived—alternative insemination—and by whom? Frozen sperm from an unknown donor or live sperm from a known donor are the current options.

For partnered lesbians, another issue presents itself. If the child is to be birthed, who is to be the biological mother? How will the roles be divided within the family? How will the coparent (nonbiological mother) feel? Can there be *two* lesbian mothers in one family in a society in which the term *lesbian mothers* is in itself an oxymoron (Lewin & Lyons, 1982, Weston, 1991)?

Lesbian coparenting may force a differentiation in roles, by virtue of both personality and circumstance, that many lesbians have resisted or rejected in the traditional heterosexual family (McCandlish, 1987). Practicing clinicians, among others working with and thinking about families, recognize the mythic character of the "traditional" family, heterosexual or otherwise. Yet there exists in the culture a loosely constructed map of the heterosexual family from which families may deviate. These same maps do not exist for gay and lesbian families (Caspar, Shultz, & Wickens, 1992).

## francis and barrie

Much to her surprise, Francis felt very possessive of her baby daughter Emma and resented, against her better judgment, her partner Barrie's claim of being Emma's mother too. Francis wanted very much for them to be a family, for Barrie to coparent Emma with her. But another mother . . . could a baby really have two mothers?

Francis was in her mid-thirties when she decided to become pregnant through alternative insemination by an unknown donor. She and Barrie had been together for three years, but Barrie remained ambivalent about the relationship, unsure whether it was one to which she wanted to make a life commitment. Feeling the pressure of her biological clock, Francis went ahead and got pregnant. Barrie had always wanted children and Francis's persistence and determination to create a family seemed to push Barrie into the commitment that Francis was looking for. Barrie was immensely supportive during the pregnancy, though Francis seemed somewhat depressed and withdrawn.

Barrie was bemused and disquieted at Francis's withdrawal, missing the intimacy that they had had, an intimacy that she had hoped would deepen around the baby's arrival. Instead, they seemed to drift apart. Barrie was hoping to stimulate her breasts to lactate and breastfeed Emma so that she could share in the experience and offer some relief to Francis, and to equalize her status as Emma's *real* mother. Francis agreed in theory, but, in practice, every time Barrie allowed Emma to suck on her breast Francis left the room tangled in a web of hurt, jealousy, and rage.

Barrie was in a quandary. After all, she wasn't Emma's *real* mother; she hadn't carried her nor suffered the pains of labor; legally she had no rights to the child. She could only be Emma's mother if Francis conferred that status upon her. Barrie abandoned her attempts to breastfeed Emma.

Like many coparents in similar situations (one biological and the other not), Barrie was hypervigilant to every sign of Emma's preference for one parent or the other (McCandlish, 1987). For the most part, Barrie felt fully bonded with her daughter; she loved and was "in love" with the wonder that was Emma. But her confidence as a mother was continually eroded by her partner's reluctance to share—not parenthood, but motherhood. Here, gender served to define a unique status for Francis that she was loathe to surrender.

Barrie's gendered body identity had always been somewhat problematic. Her mother had always and continued to criticize the ways in which she deviated from an idealized version of the heterosexual female: Barrie's breasts were too small, her body too hairy; she wore no make-up; she dressed poorly. Terrified that her lesbianism had rendered her somewhat mutant, Barrie dreamed of damaged or alien bodies. Unconsciously, this failed body was represented by what Barrie referred to as "lesbian mutant," with mis-shapened alien body parts and other gross deformities.

There was enormous tension and dissension generated in the relationship around this maternal ambiguity and competition, which, without both the support of other lesbians undergoing similar stresses (they were part of a lesbian mothers/babies group) and couples' therapy, might have rent the relationship.

### tricia and manuela

Tricia was unable to conceive. She was perimenopausal midway into her forties; she felt this not only as an enormous loss but also—and despite her knowing to the contrary—as proof that there was something very wrong with her. Manuela gave birth to a beautiful baby girl, but Tricia's happiness was compromised by her worries that she was not the baby's *real* mother, that she in fact was not a real mother and couldn't be because of some endogenous flaw of her reproductive system as well as a gender flaw—a glitch in her womanhood that would inevitably be discovered by her daughter.

Feeding the baby became a problem for the couple, which had serious repercussions on their relationship. Tricia found her partner's breastfeeding of their baby excruciatingly painful; it stimulated a morass of envy and hatred (self- and other directed) that was difficult to contain. Manuela resented Tricia's incursion on her maternal pleasure: the guilt that was induced by Tricia's envy and her displaced attacks on the mother who had "deprived" her of a a fertile and fruitful body.

Unlike Francis above, Manuela was unambivalent about her daughter having two mothers. She welcomed almost every aspect of Tricia's mothering and objected only out of her sense of anxiety that everything be done perfectly—that is, her way! Learning to tolerate different parenting styles, however, is very different from learning to accommodate two parents who are not differentiated by socially legitimized gender roles and are hence more vulnerable to a certain form of competition.

## lesbian families

New lesbian families have, for the most past, yet to reach the consulting room. The children are too young to evidence major difficulties and have yet to be studied systematically. Support groups within the community have proved inordinately successful in helping women and couples decide on how to make their family—adoption, alternative fertilization, known or unknown donor.

However, many lesbian couples enter treatment as they begin to confront these issues. Most specifically, if it is to be a biological offspring, who will birth the child? How will the coparent feel? What are the issues of jealousy and exclusion for her? Can a child really have two mommies? Issues of role often surface individually here for each partner and as the couple examines the parts that they may have been unconsciously enacting. (Who is the caretaker, and who is to be taken care of? Who is the butch and who is the femme? Is one more of "real girl" and, if so, is she the one to be the "mommy "? But this child is to have two mommies, and how can they be so very different?)

Lesbians, too, can be locked into the narrow gender binaries that the culture proscribes.

In the last two decades, many women have left traditional heterosexual marriages to form homosexual unions and have, when the courts allowed, brought their children with them. Like their heterosexual counterparts, these step-families have a variety of constellations, with varied arrangements of custody and coparenting responsibility.

For the mother who leaves a traditional marriage, her sexuality is flagrantly an issue in a way it never need be for a heterosexual woman. Traditional patriarchal culture has rejected the notion of a woman subject for whom sexuality and nurturance are not in opposition. Lesbians born of that culture have internalized those splits so that they may remain fearful that their sexuality negates motherhood. Moreover, by raising their children in an obviously more difficult life style, they opt for the fulfillment of their needs, the actualization of their desire, in a way that casts them irreparably outside the realm of object/other, which is so often synonymous with being Mother (Bassin, Honey, & Kaplan, 1994).

For new lesbian mothers, the decision to initiate parenting is often experienced as profoundly reparative when there is a new sense of connectedness and partial identification with an identity as an adult woman nurturer, replacing a prior de-identification with mother as female. There is less guilt, less questioning of one's adequacy as an adult, and a more positive embrace of one's gender as restrictions have in fact been diminished. Less anger and guilt toward the actual mother will often initiate a positive spiral of interactions so that a real as well as a psychic rapprochement between mother and daughter often occurs.

For the lesbian step-family, the initiation of lesbian parenting is often more conflictual. For the newly lesbian mother, the open change in sexual preference presents her with a seeming rejection of both her parents: a father/man to take as a primary love object; a heterosexual mother/woman with whom to identify. Feelings of depression and loss are accompanied by guilt. Initially, these affects can be masked by the joys of a new love affair and the exhilarating feeling of having finally embraced a more authentic subjectivity. As the difficulties of being a lesbian family are confronted, there is frequently an ensuing depression over the loss of heterosexual privilege in the external world, which coincides with the loss of internal objects within.

Feelings of shame and guilt are often expressed by new lesbian mothers in relation to parenting. Parents struggle with coming out to their children, fearful that they will be rejected as they have seemingly rejected their own internal objects. Retaliation is expected from children, as it is expected from archaic superego figures revived in the belated working through of sexual issues. For many women in this critical period, sexuality becomes confused with autonomy, as the expression of homosexual desire is confused with individuation from the maternal imago.

No matter what the origin of the lesbian family, there are certain social stressors that all eventually face (Crawford, 1987). Most marked is a sense of isolation and/or invisibility; although the number of lesbian and gay families is on the increase, they are still a rare phenomenon, deviant in both the heterosexual and homosexual communities. Parenting forces lesbians to interact with the traditional heterosexual and often heterosexist educational, medical, and religious institutions. Each and every interaction raises the problem of presentation and reception. How shall we present ourselves? How will we be received? Do we want to identify ourselves as a lesbian family? Can we, should we, make these decisions for our children, and what might the consequences be?

However, and it cannot be stressed strongly enough, although there are problems unique to gay and lesbian families, most families seeking help in clinical settings are there for the same reasons as other families. We do our lesbian and gay families a grave injustice if we assume that sexuality is *the* issue, either causal or correlative, just as we do our individual patients or analysands a similar injustice if we assume anything about their sexuality, life style, or the interrelationship of these with their presenting problems simply because of their being lesbian.

## notes

1. Failed generativity, according to Erikson (1985), results in regressions to earlier stages and is manifest in an obsessive need for pseudo-intimacy or a compulsive kind of preoccupation with self-imagery—both with a pervading sense of stagnation.

2. For a fuller discussion of the place of recognition in sexual subjectivity, see Benjamin (1988).

3. For a fuller discussion of the relationship between true self and sexuality, see "coming out/being heard" in this volume.

4. Levinson (1978), in his study of male adulthood, seized on the importance of mentors and mentoring in generative development, while recognizing that women are rarely mentors themselves. According to Levinson, mentoring utilizes the parenting impulse but is more complex and requires some degree of mid-life individuation. Moreover, "the mentor is doing something for himself. He is making productive use of his own knowledge and skill in middle age. It leads him to accept other burdens of his generation—exercising authority, providing leadership, making decisions that will have significant consequence for a widening circle of others" (pp. 253–254).

In a brief note, Levinson attributes the lack of women mentors as a function of their difficulty in just surviving in the work force. But mentoring, as Levinson has defined it, refers to traditionally male areas of leadership and authority in the public arena. Women have rarely been mentors, especially to men. Historically, they have rarely been permitted to be (Kantor, 1977), while internally they often feel anxiety and conflict around assuming such roles (Person, 1982).

5. One path to lesbian sexuality as theorized by Eisenbud (1982).

6. For an interesting reading of this paper, see Adrienne Harris (1991).

7. The developmental origins of such an identity are discussed in a "lesbian is . . . a lesbian is not," in this volume.

8. There are currently between one million and five million lesbian mothers and between one million and three million gay fathers in the United States. An estimated six million to 14 million children have a lesbian or gay parent. An estimated 10,000 children are being raised by lesbians who became pregnant through artificial insemination. See Singer & Descamps (1994), p. 36; Patterson (1992), pp. 1025–1042.

9. The Gay Pride March, June 1994.

10. As of 1994, six states permitted adoption by same-sex couples. Most adoptions by gay or lesbian couples are officially recorded as single-parent adoptions (Singer & Descamps, 1994, p. 36).

# deconstructing and
# reconstructing motherhood*

The "body" is breaking up. . . . In postmodernity,
even the organs are separating from the body. That
these organs are literal makes them no less organs
of power. The womb is disjunct from the breast,
for example, the vagina from the mouth that
speaks, the ovaries and their production form the
womb, etc. The lesbian body's relation to these reified technologies is entirely representative of the
contradictions of lesbian subject positions in postmodernity. While new reproductive technologies
generally reinforce a repressive straight economy
of maternal production, body management, and
class-privileged division of labor, the technology of
cross uterine egg transplants finally allows a lesbian to give birth to another lesbian's child.

—GRIGGERS, *"The Age of (Post)*
*Mechanical Reproduction"*

*Portions of this paper appeared in Thoughts on the Constructions of Maternal
Representations, *Psychoanalytic Psychology*, *Vol. 10*(3) (Summer 1993) [Special issue:
Women, Psychoanalysis and Gender, Adria E. Schwartz & Donna Bassin, eds.]; and
Taking the Nature Out of Mother, in D. Bassin, M. Honey, & M. Kaplan, eds.,
*Representations of Motherhood*, New Haven: Yale University Press, 1994.

The culture's commitment to and investment in reproduction technology in the past thirty years has shaken the very foundation of our notions of motherhood. The use of fertilization aids, ovulatory tracking, alternative insemination, in vitro fertilization, and surrogacy have cast a long shadow over the "naturalness" of the reproductive process. Thus, there has been a radical shift from the notion of Mother and Motherhood to mothering ones. It is a shift that reflects an active identity that exists within a temporal frame that transcends gender. It is a relational entity and one whose subjectivity is implicit. Freed from the bonds of discrete gender sex roles, we can begin to think of mothering in a far more complex and textured fashion, occurring as it does in a continuum of multiple subjectivities and relations.

On August 14, 1990, Anna Johnson, a 29-year-old pregnant surrogate mother, filed suit in a California state court for the custody of the child she was carrying, a genetic offspring of Mark and Crispina Calvert. The Calverts had donated sperm and ova to create an embryo that was then transferred from a petrie dish in the laboratory to the womb of Ms. Johnson, the single parent of a three year old. She was to turn the baby over to the Calverts for $10,000. At the time of the filing, the baby was to be due in two months. Johnson—like Elizabeth Kane (a pseudonym), the first known woman to sign a legal contract for surrogacy, and Mary Beth Whitehead-Gould, genetic and gestational mother of Baby M—attempted to renege and claim her parental rights. In the case of Ana Johnson, the court denied that right, ruling that the child she was carrying had "no biological relation to her" (based on her lack of genetic connection) and that therefore Johnson must be looked upon as a "foster parent" providing a temporary home via her womb. They denied her claims to motherhood by devaluing her gestational relation to the child and likening her uterus to a temporary fetal shelter.[1]

In that same month, another article appeared in the *New York Times* hailing recent advances in bioengineering that would open the doors of motherhood to postmenopausal women through in vitro fertilization with donated ova. In that case, it seems, the medical profession assumes that the gestational mother is to be the *real* mother, and the genetically connected mother who was legitimized by the Court in the Johnson case is to be reduced to the status of "anonymous donor."

The culture's commitment to and investment in reproductive technology in the past thirty years seems to have taken the nature out of Mother Nature. The development and use of fertilization aids, ovulatory tracking with its concomitant opportunity for gender selection, alternative insemination, in vitro fertilization, and surrogacy, have cast a long shadow over the "naturalness" of the reproductive process. Mother Nature can no longer be counted upon as the arbiter of fertility, the provider of care. Neither nature nor mothers can be assumed to be what they were, and what they are forms the province of substantial debate.

Just as arguments about the essentialist versus social constructionist views of gender/motherhood have comprised much of the discourse within feminist theory, so has it been the subtext in much of the psychological writing about women/motherhood as well.[2] Although women's mothering and their reproductive capacities have often been used as ammunition in the arsenals of the opposing camps, the subjects of mothers and motherhood have rarely stood as the object of analysis in and of itself.

As reproductive technology developed and entered the mass culture, our theoretical inadequacies became glaringly obvious. We now struggle to understand the changes in our thinking about mothers, mothering, and motherhood. Through a discussion of some of the problematics raised by issues of surrogacy as illustrative of the technologizing of reproduction, and a through a brief look at Margaret Atwood's *The Handmaid's Tale* as feminist parable, I hope to highlight the inadequacy of the essentialist/social constructionist polarity as a vehicle of analysis.

## will the real mother please stand up?

The question of the relationship of kinship to motherhood is not new. For thousands of years, cultures have had adoptions whereby the "biological" or "natural" mother has given up her offspring to be raised by an adoptive mother. Here, natural or real is equated with biological. But with advances in biotechnology, we have increased possibilities: the genetic mother (donator of the ova), the gestational or birth mother, the adoptive or social mother. Even surrogacy is distinguished by whether it is traditional or not.

In traditional surrogacy, a male donates sperm for alternative insemination to a surrogate who is the genetic mother to the ensuing offspring. In gestational surrogacy, the surrogate is not genetically related to the offspring, but has become pregnant through in vitro fertilization.

The year 1978 marked the first birth of a child (Louise Brown) conceived through in vitro fertilization. Since that time, and despite the fact that 90 percent of in vitro fertilizations fail (Rothman, 1989a), as many as 10,000 embryos are frozen by women each year for future use (A. Schwartz, 1994).

Medicine seems to have developed ARTs (current acronym for alternative reproductive technologies) for heterosexuals suffering from infertility problems, but lesbians and gay men have—and continue to make—an enormous change in who and what is considered a family.

An estimated 10,000 children are being raised by lesbians who became pregnant through artificial insemination.[3]

ARTs technologies have allowed women to reject the biological constraints of heterosexuality and the institution of marriage as the exclusive pathway to motherhood. The associative link between women, marriage, fertility, and motherhood is being eroded, if not broken, in the laboratory. The traditional shame of barrenness, the inevitible sterility of menopause, the onerous ticking of the biological clock, the very legitimation of womanhood by reproductive function, are all called into question by alternative modes of reproductive technologies. In this way, our increased knowledge of reproductive functioning and the technology that has been created in the service of that knowledge, liberate women from their bodies and from their history of objectification and exclusive identification with motherhood and nurturance. Alternative paths to motherhood seem to offer previously disenfranchised groups new options while allowing women even greater control over their bodies and how they are to be used.

Let us look for a moment to the now famous case of Baby M, a trial that captured the nation's attention and split the feminist community asunder as the phenomenon of paid surrogacy focused the public's attention on how technology could call motherhood into question. The case of Baby M was and continues to be (with multiple variations of surrogacy and adoption arrangements) the focus of debate because it raises fundamental questions as to the meaning of motherhood within the culture. Is it a right of ownership, and, if so, upon what is that based? Is motherhood a relationship of caring or caretaking? Is it an instinct or a mandate? Is motherhood a construction of femininity or constitutive of womanhood?

In 1986, Mary Beth Whitehead, wife of a sanitation worker and the mother of two, agreed to be artifically inseminated by William Stern, to bear the child thus conceived, and to deliver that child to William and Elizabeth Stern for the contractually agreed upon sum of $10,000.

Elizabeth Stern, a pediatrician, claimed to have self-diagnosed multiple sclerosis and thus felt a pregnancy to be life endangering. Mary Beth Whitehead was to act as Elizabeth's surrogate in the creation of the Stern family.

Toward the end of her pregnancy, Mary Beth Whitehead became convinced that she could not give up her baby. She had made a grave mistake and vowed to keep the child. The Sterns, as well as a great proportion of the American population, were outraged that Mary Beth felt she could so blatantly ignore or violate the terms of a legal contract. She was legally bound. The fact that she promised to return all monies received and forfeit those promised made no difference. The fact that it is elementary in contract law that performance may not be enforced, but merely that damages can be collected made no difference. By threatening to keep her child, Mary Beth proved herself to be indubitably outside the moral pale: first, by offering to sell her child, and then by changing her mind and trying to keep it. Clearly she was an unstable and unfit mother.

It seemed we were back in King Solomon's court as Mary Beth kidnapped her baby and kept her hidden from the Sterns; then the Sterns, in conjunction with "the authorities," stole the baby back and returned it to the jurisdiction of the court, which in turn delivered the baby back to them.

At the initial trial, where the Sterns sought to terminate all parental rights to "the surrogate," one of their expert witnesses, psychologist Lee Salk, informed the court;

> I don't see that there were any "parental rights" that existed in the first place. As I see it . . . Mr. Stern and Mrs. Whitehead entered into an agreement that was clearly understoood by both. The agreement involved the provision of ovum by Mrs. Whitehead for artificial insemination in exchange for ten thousand dollars . . . and so my feeling is that in both structural and functional terms, Mr. and Mrs.

> Stern's role as parents was achieved by *a surrogate uterus and not a sur-*
> *rogate mother.* (Chessler, 1989, p. 231; italics mine)[4]

In this surrogacy arrangement, Elizabeth Stern was able to transcend her alleged biological limitations (the multiple sclerosis) and achieve motherhood by virtue of her relation to Baby M's genetic father and, presumably, by caring for and "mothering" the child.

But for Mary Beth, the situation is quite different. Far from being liberated from her body, in the state's eye Mary Beth Whitehead becomes her body, or rather a disembodied part-object, an instrumental construct to fulfill the needs of a man who wishes a genetic offspring. If she is only her body—or rather a body part—then she cannot be a mother.

In the preliminary surrogacy agreement signed by both, William Stern is referred to as the "natural father" or "natural and biological father" while Mary Beth Whitehead is referred to exclusively as the "surrogate" (Chessler, 1989). Here, it seems, only the male is held to be privy to nature, the woman having sold her claim for $10,000. Clearly the womb is no longer considered essential to the biological process of reproduction. It is merely a temporary shelter that will no doubt soon be replicated or subsumed by reproductive technological advance.

So who is the real mother of Baby M? Mary Beth Whitehead, of whose flesh she is, who conceived and carried her, who offered to sell her for a goodly sum of money? Elizabeth Stern, mostly silent through-out the prolonged media circus that accompanied the trials, who did not wish to bear the risks of childbirth but who claimed to want and love Baby M? The trial evoked tremendous passion on both sides, with essentialists championing women's biological rights to motherhood and social constructionists rejoicing at their liberation from the primitive bonds of women's reproductive capacities.

Not surprisingly, the state delimited the discourse. There was no dis-cussion about the possibility of Baby M having two mothers in legal parity, two mothers who are equally valued, without one being "realer," more primary than the other. Traditionally this has not been an option, as the court recognizes only one legal father and one legal mother; there is an unspoken moral purview. A child is to be conceived from a monogamous heterosexual union, and the value of that union is to be indemnified by the court.

Should it have been possible for both Elizabeth Stern and Mary Beth Whitehead to be Baby M's mother(s)? Might not they be awarded equal access to and time with Baby M and share equally in all decisions concerning her upbringing, as in traditional joint-custody divorce cases?

But what of the psychological ramifications: Can a child have two mothers? Psychoanalysis has been struggling over the past ten years in its shift from a one-person to a two-person psychology, from a classical, intrapsychically focused theory to a relational theory with its interpersonal, intersubjective, and object relations components, resulting in an increased emphasis on the mother/infant dyad as the cradle of selfhood.[5] How might relational theory accommodate the basic triad of one infant/two mothers that might occur had the court awarded joint custody to Elizabeth Stern and Mary Beth Whitehead-Gould?

Neither classical Freudian-based theory nor relational theory has addressed itself to alternative families, where there can be no automatic presumption as to who or what it means to be the mother: genetic, gestational, adoptive, lesbian coparents. Theoreticially, it would require the abandonment of the oedipal stage as the heart of the psychosexual develpmental matrix. At the least, notions of dyad and triads have to be substituted for the structures of mother-child, mother/father-child, that seem so fundamental to the heterosexual concept of family (A. Schwartz, 1986). The idea of two mothers challenges the constructs of "positive" and "negative" oedipal configurations, where a boy's choice of father as primary libidinal object or a girl's choice of her mother is viewed as inverted, cast as a "negative" oedipal situation, and often viewed as an indication of failed attempts to master the positive oedipal conflicts.[6] Moreover, the very basis for identification would be shaken as gender would no longer be conflated with sexuality, and Jones (1927) choice—to either *have* the object or *be* it—would no longer be viable.

Our legal system, embedded in a "naturally" heterosexual matrix, has maintained that there can be only one mother.[7] There is no continued legal recognition of the birth mother, who is most often the genetic and gestational mother, in the adoptee's life. The state prefers to eradicate the birth mother; after an adoption becomes legal, the newborn infant's birth certificate lists the adoptive parent as mother while the birth mother's name is sealed in the court's records and lost to the child, possibly forever. Although this procedure was purportedly instituted in order to protect the birth mother and insure the integrity of the adoptive family, it also serves to reaffirm sexual conservancy: babies are not born outside of marriage; mothers do not give up their babies.

Regarding Baby M., the New Jersey Supreme Court restored the parental rights to Mary Beth Whitehead-Gould that were terminated in a lower court, but allowed the Sterns to keep custody in "the best interests of the child." In this case, parental rights guaranteed visitation, but the Stern's custody and the distances involved virtually preclude shared decision making by the mothers.

This case was one of the most journalistically popular in the years of 1987 and 1988, and in the early to mid-'90s the popular culture was rife with filmed versions of "true life" tragedies of "natural" and adoptive families struggling over who are the "real" parents. Surrogacy cases in particular not only raise fundamental issues about the culture's changing attitudes toward mothers, mothering, and motherhood, but also, as Harold Cassidy, Mary Beth's lawyer pointed out, unearth the subterranean issues of class and caste so rarely addressed in popular American discourse. "What we are witnessing, and what we can predict will happen, is that one class of Americans will exploit another class. And it will always be the wife of the sanitation worker who must bear the children for the pediatrician" (Chessler, 1989, p. 160).

Barbara Katz Rothman (1988, 1989b) has written extensively about what she terms the "commodification of motherhood." According to Rothman (1989b), we have become victims of an ideology that treats people as objects, commodities for sale, and the fetus as a product subject to quality control. Women (and men) are treated as producers without emotional ties to their products. Women sell their ova and rent their wombs. She suggests that surrogate mothers who are content with their role "have accepted the alienation of the worker from the product of her labor; the baby like any other commodity does not belong to the producer but to the purchaser" (1988, p. 99). In this analysis, surrogates who recant ultimately can not accept this commodification of their motherhood.

Rothman decries an ideology where the relation of a mother to her own body is no longer esteemed and suggests that the valuation of genetics over the gestational relation operates primarily as a boon to the baby brokers. The elevation to primacy of the gestational relation that Rothman demands is surely to undo women's growing alienation from her body, its further commodification and objectification. In her more recent writing, Rothman (1994) states clearly that she rejects traditional kinship ties with their claims to ownership. She rejects surrogacy because in her analysis it negates interpersonal relationships in the service of mercantilism.

While Rothman blasts the evil of reproductive technology as an alienating representative of our commodity culture, Bassin (1989) argues that reproductive technology may be situationally traumatic without necessarily being symbolic or carrying negative psychological impact to the integrity of the self. Citing clinical material, Bassin suggests that reproductive technology may be experienced as alienating or not, depending on one's subjectivity. Another way of approaching that question might be to ask: Is it possible for science and technology to stand outside the berth of ideology, or is one's comfort with the constraints of ideology dependent on one's psychic structure?

This is where the seas divide between lesbians and traditionally heterosexually identified married women. Women in the latter category, to whom Bassin, refers, struggle not only with their own internalization of society's conflation of motherhood and femininity but are also most often dealing clinically with the deflation of their narcissistic fantasies of perfection and their identification/competition with their own idealized mothers. For lesbians (and some heterosexually identified single women, as well) alternative insemination by anonymous or known donors allows for the actualization of their maternal fantasies and eliminates the necessity for the relinquishment of their sexual subjectivity in the service of their femininity.

### clinical anecdote

After considerable thought and with much trepidation, Paula announced to her very traditional mother that she and her lover wished to start a family and that she was hoping to become pregnant by alternative insemination. Mother was appalled and argued in an anticipated fashion that it "just wasn't right," that it was against "God's way," that she could never accept such a child as her real grandchild. This possibly understandable though hurtful response—given the mother's sociocultural milieu—became suspect, however, when Mother suggested that her daughter let her lover become pregnant. "She should have the baby, not you." Her relationship with her mother had always been problematic for Paula, who felt that whenever the specter of happiness appeared within reach, the mother would find some way to "pull the rug out from under her" or "knock the wind out of her sails." Growing up in the 1950s, Mother had been a traditional homemaker who seemed resentful and somewhat devaluing of her secondary role as wife and mother—while guarding it jealously.

In this case, Mother's rejection of her lesbian daughter's intention to become pregnant really revolved around her *envy* of the possibility of her daughter's "having her cake and eating it too." She could gain the status of being a mother without having to be a wife.

## the handmaid's tale

Margaret Atwood's novel, *The Handmaid's Tale* (1987) appears to embody a strange admixture of Rothman's concern for women's increasing alienation from her body and the exploitation of her reproductive capacities, coupled with a nightmarish vision of an essentialist feminism gone awry. In some ways a classic feminist dystopia, *The Handmaid's Tale*, tells of a time where a return to militaristic, Protestant fundamentalism born of an environmental apocalypse has created a society where reproduction is considered the sole province and responsibility of women. Toxic contamination has rendered most women and men infertile, although men, in keeping with the idealization of their powers and the concomitant splitting of sexuality and reproduction, are never presumed to be so. The handmaids act as surrogates, a class of women whose sole function is to provide offspring for infertile couples. Elizabeth Kane's personal story echoes Atwood's vision as she declares, "We have become a society that demands instant gratification, and now we are demanding instant babies by expecting healthy women to become our breeding stock. The fact that our society has accepted using breeders to create children for wealthy people frightens me" (Kane, 1988, p. 64).

*The Handmaid's Tale* takes place in the Republic of Gilead, a small section of the country located in what might be New England, given the reference to the Salem Witch trials; but as Aunt Lydia (the prototype for the co-opted woman, who embraces her oppressor and willingly passes on that oppression in the name of love) so wisely repeats to her young charges, "The Republic of Gilead knows no bounds. Gilead is within you" (Atwood, 1987, p. 187). As the handmaid tells us, in Gilead, women are valued and caste solely for their reproductive capacities. Fertility determines one's usefulness to a society that discards or exiles lower class women—unwomen—who have been unwilling or unable to bear fruit for the ruling elite of commanders and their wives. The handmaids have generic names only: they *are* their function. The Marthas serve; they are domestic servants who are too old to reproduce or who, in one case, had a tubal ligation before it had become illegal.

The handmaids, the lucky fertile ones, are called Ofglen, Ofwarren. They have no identity other than that of reproductive appendices to the men they are temporarily servicing. Dressed in red (a reference to Hawthorne's *Scarlet Letter*), they are spoken about as vessels. In a wonderful touch in the book, it is noted that the wives have forbidden the use of face cream or lotion for the handmainds—They are considered vanities. "We are containers, it's only the insides of our bodies that are important. The outside can become hard and wrinkled, for all they care, like the shell of a nut . . . they don't want us to look attractive" (Atwood, 1987, p. 124). The aunts—the women who imprison, train, and condition other women—tell them they are a national resource. And there is envy and false competition among them for parturition. But mostly there is shame and despair and for those who could remember other times, a longing for personhood and a self that existed independent of the uterus they have become.

What is so interesting about Margaret Atwood's treatment of the problematic of the relationship of women to their reproductive capacities is that she demonstrates, in a most harrowing fashion, the ways in which we can pervert a position through its radical extension. Overvaluation of the biological potential of women to bear young, and then finding that reproductive potential to be constituitive of womanhood, leads ultimately to the objectification of woman as body/nature and to the obliteration of her subjectivity. Alternatively, as women seek to transcend the constraints of a biologically determined existence, we risk the disembodied commodification and exploitation of our bodily selves.

Ultimately, Atwood finds the condition of patriarchy pre-emptive of even the formulation of that contradiction. There is only one woman who retains her name throughout the narrative: Moira. Moira is a resister from the outset. She attempts many escapes from the Red Center (the training ground for the handmaids), and is captured, beaten, and finally remanded to work at Jezebel's, a brothel servicing the ruling class of men. Is the irony here that Moira is a lesbian and therefore a longstanding resister (Rich, 1981)? Or that, given the choice of how to service men in our patriarchy—sexually or through reproduction—she chooses her sexuality as a more secure means of retaining some measure of autonomy, integrity, and wholeness? In either case, Atwood seems to say that it is the historical condition of patriarchy that defines what a women or a mother is, and that there can be no truly feminist conception until that condition is removed.

Similarly, feminist theorist Ann Snitow asks, "To what extent is motherhood a powerful identity? . . . To what extent is it a patriarchal construction that inevitably places mothers outside the realm of social, the changing, the active?" (Snitow, 1989, p. 49). In Atwood's novel, female existence is defined and circumscribed by one's relation to Motherhood. Is it possible, Snitow asks, for biological difference to wither away as a basis for social organization, or are the sexes endurably different biologically and therefore psychically requiring different cultural organization?

## psychoanalysis and motherhood

For Freud and his disciples within classical psychoanalysis, the psychology of motherhood rested on a foundation of anatomy and desire. Freud (1925, 1933) proclaims a fundamental though not totally inflexible biological determinism in psychosexual development and describes what he assumes to be the likely progression of the young girl toward femininity/heterosexuality and the wish to have a baby, based largely on the child's perception of the obvious and universal superiority of the penis. Thus, the realization and acknowledgment of the anatomical differences between the sexes propels the pre-oedipal girl to abandon her mother as a primary love object, renounce her active/clitoral "masculine" sexuality and embrace her passive/vaginal "feminine" sexuality, that can produce a baby as its consolation prize.

Subsequent psychoanalysts have pointed out that Freud had mistaken the concrete anatomic penis for a culturally privileged phallus, that girls seem to have an early awareness and positive valuation of their own genitals that is not reactive to a phallic stance, and that Freud was wrong about the importance of the so-called oedipal stage in the development of female gender role identity (Fliegel, 1973, 1982; Grossman & Stewart, 1976; Kleeman, 1976; A. Schwartz, 1984a). But these claims for a girl's primary femininity still retain an essentialist bias that will again lead us to a conclusion that women are mothers because they are anatomically female. That is, their mothering will ultimately be equated with their reproductive capacities.

Chodorow (1978), in an attempt at a feminist revision of Freud's original formulation, utilizes an object relations structure to ask why women mother. What psychological operations occur to ensure the reproduction of mothering by females in our culture? Basing her theory on the psychological consequences of a culturally structured asymmetry of parenting, she deals with processes of identification and internalization, but her frame of reference is a traditionally mimetic gender/sexed model of heterosexuality comprised of two-parent nuclear families where traditionally feminine mothers give birth to and care for the young who are sired by traditionally non-nurturant masculine fathers. Like Freud (1931), Chodorow explains that girls are more likely to have a continued and intense pre-oedipal relationhsip with their mothers, their heterosexual orientation is always internally triangular, requiring a child for its emotional completion (Chodorow, 1978, p. 207). Moreover, according to Chodorow, the asymmetry of parenting raises men who are emotionally constricted, fearful of their relational needs, isolated, competitive, and hence unsatisfactory companions for most women.

Where does that leave lesbians? In the only direct reference in the book, Chodorow says, "Lesbian relationships do tend to recreate mother-daughter emotions and connections, but most women are heterosexual" (1978, p. 200). She almost seems to imply as well that women's emotional preference for being with other women is understandable but not viable, and thus handily dismisses them. It is as if no mothers were lesbians, and lesbians didn't choose to mother.

Chodorow falls within the purview of traditional psychoanalytic writings in that motherhood becomes enmeshed in female identity, and that not wanting a baby, by inference, is caught up in masculine identifications or poor bonding experiences with one's own mother. Moreover, Chodorow's theory fails to tell us how it is that some men assume the role of primary caretakers and nurturers. Clinical experience tells us that in many families it may be the man who is felt to be real nurturer even though he does not take on the usual domestic responsibilities. Who is the mother there? How might Chodorow's model apply in gay male families, where both men take equal parenting responsibilities, or where roles are divided along more traditional expressive and instrumental paramenters? Would the male children in such families become the nurturers and females the repressed, nonrelational ones, in reaction to their positional identifications as "not-like" their primary caretaker?[8]

As compared to Freud and the ensuing arena of classical psychoanalysis, however, the object relations school of psychoanalytic thinking does contain the roots of a more flexible, less essentialist understanding of development, based as it is on the strength and influence of early caretaking dyads that need not be gender specific nor gender continuous. It is within these early caretaking dyads that internalizations evolve that are historical, idiosyncratic, and dependent on the confluence of mothering styles and the congenital/temporal needs of the infant.

If one looks to Winnicott as the object relations theorist who dealt most specifically with mothering, we find him speaking in actuality of early "mothering work," where mother is the provider of the facilitating environment, a good-enough mother who is able to *hold* the infant (protect from physiological insult, take account of the infant's various tactile and kinesthetic sensitivities, and accommodate to the infant's rhythms) and mirror appropriately to provide the ground for ego relatedness and a sense of going-on-being.

In his essay on the parent-infant relationship, Winnicott (1960) divides the functions of the parents along traditionally gendered lines in keeping with the socioeconomic custom of his milieu. Mother cares for the infant while father cared for the mother by protecting her environment. There is however, no sustained discussion of "fathering work" as it relates specifically to development, nor any reason to suppose that men are any less able to provide a facilitating environment than women. Unlike Chodorow, who tells us specifically that our patterns of asymmetrical parenting reproduce women who mother and men who do not, because the men have repressed the relational/nurturant aspects of themselves that are female identified, Winnicott tends not to deal as systematically with issues of gender or sexual difference (Chodorow, 1978).[9] With Winnicott, as with other British object relations theorists—and Kohut and fellow American self-psychologists—we are left with theories describing internalized object relations and the development of the self that are essentially genderless—not by intent, but by omission.

### is motherhood a gendered relation?

The postmodern critique of feminist theory questions the very primacy of sexual difference as a field of inquiry. Focusing on male-female difference obscures other issues, such as power relations, and assumes that unitary categories of male/female are vaild ones. Snitow (1989) speaks of the "divide" that keeps forming in feminist thought between the need to build an identity of women and the need to dismantle the category entirely. The same can be said of motherhood where women, it seems, have always resisted being confined and defined by cultural representations of motherhood and yet are loathe to give up their mother right.

Butler (1990a) offers a provocative critique of the geneaology of gender categories in an attempt to subvert what she perceives to be the oppression of gender hierarchy and compulsory heterosexuality on our thinking. Most of what Butler questions about the category of women within feminist theory—that is, the very construction of a unitary and presumed universal category—applies to mothers and motherhood as well. As Butler attempts a deconstruction of the category of women, we might ask, in a similar vein, does the term *mother* denote a common identity, a stable signifier that commands the assent of those it purports to describe and represent? Or is the construction of the category *mother*, like that of *women*, an unwitting regulation and reification of gender relations that furthermore attains stability and coherence only in the context of a traditional heterosexual matrix? Butler's critique would suggest that the category of mother is a constructed subject based on a questionable category of gender.

Butler suggests that there is no necessity for gender to retain a mimetic relationship to sex, given that the former is presumed to be culturally constructed and the latter biological. Thus, man and masculine might just as easily signify a female body as a male one; and woman and feminine might just as easily signify a male body as a female one. Culture has always recognized this in fact, and we have always had our "masculine" women and "feminine men" with differing roles and differing levels of approbation or proscription, depending on the culture. Butler (1990a) extends her analysis even further, however, and calls into question the very distinction between a supposedly biologically given sex and a culturally constructed gender. Butler's analysis destabilizes the automatic identification of motherhood with women so that we recognize a mothering subject that is less unitary and more conditional, free of the constrictions of gender. How, then, might one identify a Mother or mothering?

Is motherhood a gendered relation? Our brief look at the problematic raised by the advent of reproduction technology and its representation in culture suggests that motherhood is a matter of relation. But just what that relation is, and who will define and legitimize it, remains unclear. Butler's analysis further complicates things, in that the very identification of motherhood with women becomes eroded if not disappeared in its entirety.

In a somewhat different vein, Ruddick (1989) introduced a concept of mothering as work that transcends gender. She distinguished between birthing labor, which only women do, and mothering work. Birthing labor remains in the special province of women, and women might choose to celebrate this, just as in a particular situation genetic parents might choose to be recognized in a specific fashion. But for Ruddick, mothers and mothering work need not be gendered:

> A mother is a person who takes on responsibility for children's lives and for whom providing child care is a significant part of her or his working life. I mean "her or his." Although most mothers have been and are women, mothering is potentially work for men and women. Although most mothers have been and are women, mothering is potentially work for men and women. This is not to deny . . . that there may be biologically based differences in styles of mothering. . . . I am suggesting that whatever difference might exist between female and male mothers, there is no reason to believe that one sex rather than the other is more capable of doing maternal work. (Ruddick, 1989, pp. 40–41)

Ruddick suggests that the push toward the ever-increasing sophistication of reproductive technology stems from envy of female reproductive capacities and the wish to strip that capacity from the exclusive province of women. This notion stands, in a way, as the inverse complement of Freud's, whereby a woman's urge to procreate stemmed ultimately from her penis envy in that oft-maligned, unconscious equation of penis = baby.

## taking the nature out of mother

In our culture, mothers/mothering no longer universally signifies a woman's essential biological relation to her child. By examining the impact of reproductive technology and its cultural reflections, and through the prism of postmodern critique, we have deconstructed the category *mother* as a "natural," biologically rooted, gendered relation to genetic offspring. What are the consequences of that deconstruction for theories of psychological development?

There are clearly consequences for our notions of femininity and womanhood as they interface with our assumptions about motherhood. By taking the Nature out of Mother, we rend a tectonic shift in our parallel assumptions about the universal meaning of menarche, menopause, and fertility within women's lives and, concomitantly, of the importance of traditional marriages and heterosexual intercourse for achieving reproductive goals.

Psychoanalytic theorists have been interested in the internalization of early maternal experience as the wellspring for the emergence of self and self-in-relation, with the implicit understanding that the experience is grounded in a traditional triangular heterosexual matrix. Its focus has been largely on the development of the child, with little emphasis on maternal subjectivity.[10] Recent developments in intersubjective theory involving patterns of attunement and the evolution of mutual recognition between the infant and mother also assume that the all-important infant/mother/caretaker dyad occurs within the context of a fairly traditional, heterosexual, triangular matrix. (Stern, 1985; Benjamin, 1988).

Benjamin, one of the first feminist psychoanalytic writers to deal extensively with maternal subjectivity, recognizes in a footnote that a large proportion of children in our culture do not grow up in families with a "mommy and daddy in stereotypical families with a conventional sexual division of labo." She maintains that this psychic structure must be understood within a context of the "dominant culture and its gender structure" (Benjamin, 1988, p. 105). Although she acknowledges that the figures of mother and fathers are cultural ideals that need not be played by biological mothers and fathers, or even by women and men, she reproduces those cultural ideals as she generates new theory and imbues the maternal with an almost predetermined lack of subjectivity.

If we could transcend our tremendous resistance to altering the traditional representations of motherhood based on our collective anger, envy, idealization, and objectification of our female mothers, then we might begin to ask some historically germane and potentially more interesting questions about being and experiencing motherhood. Given a shift in the conception of mothers and mothering from that of a unitary category of women in some biological or otherwise proprietary relationship to their offspring to one of a more fluid constellation of active maternal relations, constructed through the work of intersubjective dyads, I now pose these additional questions.

- How might we begin to think about the representation of maternal relations and their internalization?
- How might our changing conception of internalized maternal representations affect psychoanalytic practice?

## infant research

Recent trends in infant research support our thinking about mothering children as a function of relational dyads. Beebe (1986), for example, performed microanalyses of split-second mutual adjustments between four-month old infants and their mothers that were both coactive and alternating in highly sensitized attunements. Beebe posited that "early representations are based on how the infant's temporal-spatial schemas of the partner's behavioral flow fit into his or her own needs" (1986, p. 33).

One of the patterns studied by Beebe was the mutual regulation of what she termed "optimal levels of stimulation, leading to positive affective engagement" (1989, p.39). How does the infant respond when the mothering one[11] overshoots or undershoots optimal levels of stimulation and thus may appear distant, intrusive, or aversive? Apparently, an infant has a wide variety of behaviors for coping with such inevitable empathic misses. In one videotaped play observation—exemplary of what Beebe and Stern call a "chase/dodge interaction"—the mothering one failed to notice the infant's repeated attempts to disengage from the mother's efforts to secure more direct contact. In this observation, "the mother 'chased' by following the infant's head and body movements with her own head and body, pulling his arm, picking him up to re-adjust his orientation, or attempting to force his head in her direction" (p. 41). To every maternal overture, the infant dodged by moving back, ducking his head down, turning away, pulling his hand from her grasp, or becoming limp and unresponsive). Here, the chase behavior only increased the infant's aversive "dodge" behavior. Moreover, these maternal efforts seem to have interfered with the infant's capacity to remain oriented and visually attentive (p. 42). If a mothering one is consistently unable to notice and respond differentially to a range of infant affective engagement experiences, then this deficit will be reflected in the emerging representations.

What is internally represented when an infant repeatedly attempts to modulate the degree of stimulation in the maternal environment without success? Or, what if the infant's repeated attempts to engage are met with maternal avoidance? Presumably, at the least, the infant learns that her behavior does not effect changes in the environment. Beebe suggests that the schema of self as acting and the object as responding would be "inadequately internalized" (1986, p. 38).

The use of the word "inadequate" here suggests some form of developmental deficit but does not help us to understand how such a relation might be internalized in its particularity. Many psychoanalysts have called for the integration of psychoanalytic theory and infant research (Lichtenberg, 1981, 1983; Stern, 1985; Silverman, 1986, 1993). In addition to the positing of pathology or deficit originating in this earliest of mothering/infant interactions, it is the particular system of interactions between an infant and the mothering one that will be of concern to analysts in the consulting room.

Might not this relation between infant and particular mothering one be internalized in its specificity? We know that infants as young as two weeks old are able to distinguish their mothers from other caretakers and thus make discriminations of face and voice (Brazelton, 1980). And if that internalized relation is consistently significant over time, might we speculate as to the eventual repercussions on the young child's level of active initiation, creativity, sense of trust with that particular mothering one?

Beebe did suggest that to the extent that this kind of interaction is characteristic, it will contribute to early representations by providing one model of the "bad object" (Beebe, 1986, p. 41). However, because the experience of the "bad object" is a process, she hypothesized that the internalization will be of a *bad-self-in-relation-to-object*. The implicit assumption here, of course, is that the shift in "badness" will be from object to self.[12]

It is important for us to keep in mind that, in offering illustrative analyses from infant research, I am not suggesting that individual patterns of interaction observed between mothering ones and their infants (such as the chase/dodge) will be paradigmatic for most or all relationships. What I am suggesting we consider is that this intersubjective interaction over time will be internalized as a representation. Such a representation may or may not be generalizable, depending on the pervasiveness of the lack of mutual attunement in a variety of maternal functions with a variety of mothering ones.

In a paper on representations of relational patterns, Stern (1989) expanded on his earlier hypotheses (see Stern, 1985) and presented a model for the internalization of infantile relational experiences. At the stage of earliest infancy, Stern hypothesized that a specific lived interactive moment, an L-Moment, is encoded as an M-Moment, a memory, and that these M-Moments are organized into functional categories at the level of representations, R-Moments. What are the categories of M-Moments that get encoded as R-Moments and further as R-Scenarios? This, of course, is the meadow upon which psychoanalysts graze, the fodder for our sectarian pen.

Stern takes the position that no single variable (that is cognition, affect, or arousal) has more salience or holds a privileged position vis-à-vis the formation of R-Moments. Bowlby, whose work we will turn to shortly, was, in a way, father to this mode of theorizing. He saw the parameter of attachment as primary in our motivational systems and consequently the stuff of which our maternal representations are made. Bowlby (1980) defined attachment as "any form of behavior that results in a person attaining or maintaining proximity to some other clearly identified individual who is conceived of as better able to cope with the world" (p. 26). Much of the psychoanalytically informed infant research preceding Stern was in the area of attachment, where attempts were made to observe infants and young children in a variety of experimental situations and to assess their attachment styles based on what Bowlby (1980) had called the internal working model of attachment. Thus for Bowlby, internalized experiences with mothering ones are organized around parameters of attachment. But, this need not be the sole parameter.

Silverman (1993) pointed out:

> Self and object representation may be organized around the experience of responsive interactions to security needs. However, why should one assume that these interactions represent the *only* contribution. . . . In addition, this line of thinking presupposes a direct psychic representation of actual interactions without permitting the inclusion of the child's unique way of understanding parent-child interactions. The role of imagery, fantasy, defense, primitive guilt and reparation are not considered. (p. 22)

As psychoanalysts, we are interested in how the representation is organized and what determines its entrance into the internal world. According to Stern (1989), representations are of relational patterns, cumulative interactive histories, a series of repetitive interactive events that are mutually derived, though subjectively constructed. They are a function of both objective events and subjective experiences.

It is for us, as psychoanalysts, to determine both how and why the lived maternal experience is mediated so that it becomes internalized in the realm of the subjective. Freud postulated drive satisfaction, Klein, ontogenetic fantasy. As psychoanalytic theory develops increasingly from a one- to a two-person psychology, we are beginning to ask, as are the developmentalists, how the mothering one (and, for the attachment theorists, the attachment figures) affects the L-Moments that precede their encoding as M-Moments and ultimately R-Scenarios.

## internal working models

Let us return for a moment to the work of Bowlby, whose concept of the internal working model of attachment prefigures my thoughts on the construction of maternal representation. Bowlby (1980) suggested that the coherence, stability, and substance of relationships are represented by the internalized structures which he termed internal working models of attachment. It is through these models that individuals are able to perceive, plan, and act in that world (Bowlby, 1973). For Bowlby, the relationship to the attachment figure (the figure who provides security, protection, soothing, comfort, and help) is central in the development of self and object relations (Bretherton & Waters, 1985). Accessibility and responsivity are key attributes of the attachment figure, and the internal working models enable us to forecast the likeliness of a given attachment figure's availability and likeliness to respond appropriately. According to Bowlby (1973), "the model of the attachment figure and the model of the self are likely to develop so as to be complementary and mutually determining" (p. 204). Bowlby is vague on the role of fantasy in the construction of the internal working model; but it is clear that he gives great weight to lived experience as mediated through the distorting eyes and ears of immaturity. The lack of interiority in his model might account for why his work has been undervalued by so many psychoanalysts until recently, despite his having been embraced by developmentalists who have been able to create experimental situations to test out his theories.[13]

Bowlby, however, was not unaware of conflict. He recognized the operation of defensive processes. Internal working models operate outside of conscious awareness, and thus are resistant to change—But they are not impervious to maturation and experience. He recognized that individuals can and do operate with two or more working models of the same attachment figure, and with parallel and complementary models of the self. According to Bowlby, these models are likely to differ "in regard to their origin, their dominance, and the extent to which the subject is aware of them" (1973, p. 204). Incompatible models of attachment are understood as the product of incompatible interpretations of experience that may become defensively dissociated (Bowlby, 1980).

Although not identified as a member of the British object relations school per se, Bowlby has much in common with them. Fairbairn, for instance, joins Bowlby in maintaining that the human species is first and foremost object seeking, although he maintains the primacy of libidinal satisfaction within the remnants of an energic theory. Fairbairn—who, as Ghent (1989, p.198) points out, is the only psychoanalyst positing a self (the central ego) at birth—saw internalization as a defensive operation, not as a normative road map for living. That is, for Fairbairn (1952), internalization is a consequence of the defensive splitting of the maternal object and a function of ambivalence: the inability of the infant to have an object that is both good, in that it is libidinally satisfying, and bad, in that it is frustrating or fails to satisfy. In attempting to control the aggression that arises as a function of frustration, the child internalizes the mother as bad object. The internal bad object further splits into the needed or "exciting" object and the frustrating or rejecting object. Fairbairn also theorizes concomitant splits off the central ego. In Fairbairnian language, the libidinal ego connects to the exciting object and the internal saboteur relates to the rejecting object. These split-off egos (selves) become attached to the split-off object by libidinal ties, all repressed and out of consciousness. Good objects are not internalized and here is where Fairbairn, of course, differs from Freud (1917), where incorporation is a function of object loss; Klein (1952), for whom it is the good objects that are introjected; and Bowlby and Stern, who view internalization as the normative consequence of relational experience.

It seems that Bowlby's work—and in a way Fairbairn's—not only foreshadowed the work of Stern and his followers in infant research but also paralleled in a structural, if not dynamic, way the development of the relational school of psychoanalysis (Mitchell, 1988; Silverman, 1993).

Bretherton and Waters (1985), researchers in attachment theory, have pointed out that because the internal working models of self and attachment figures "are constructed out of dyadic experiences . . . closely intertwined . . . it may be preferable to speak of an internal working model of the *relationship*" (p. 12; italics added) rather than of internalization of closely paralleling models of the self and caretaking other. Moreover, they criticize the lack of information on and study of the internal working models of the attachment figures themselves. What studies there are (for example, Main, Cassidy, & Kaplan, 1985) focus primarily on the adults' childhood experiences with their own parents rather than on the ways in which the attachment figures' internal working models currently affect their relationships with their own children as lived in the here and now.

What is the impact of the adult's attachment system on the infant? How will the mothering one respond to the child's attempt to engage, to seek comfort, to cling, to take psychic space? And what determines those responses? Just as psychoanalysis has failed to deal with maternal subjectivity (Benjamin, 1988), so until quite recently has attachment research failed to deal with the internal working models of the attachment figures.

It seems we've come full circle now, back to the import of Stern's and Beebe's research, which is illustrative of the minute, omnipresent, feedback system originating in earliest infancy between mothering one and child. This interactive look is internalized as some mix of objective events and subjective experience (Stern, 1989, p. 55). The parameters of that loop, of course, will vary in intensity and focus given both the immediate and the developmental needs of the child, and they covary as they mesh with the particulars of the mothering relationship within a given developmental period.

Main, Kaplan, and Cassidy (1985) suggested that "Internal working models of relationships also will provide rules for the direction and organization of attention and memory, rules that permit or limit the individual's access to certain forms of knowledge regarding the self, the attachment figure, and the relationship between the self and the attachment figure. These rules will be reflected in the organization of thought and language as it relates directly and indirectly to attachment. Many will be unconscious" (p. 77).

Encoded in the empathic/recognition response will be megabytes of information about the mother's conscious and unconscious feelings about separation and autonomy, bodily competence and jouissance in its broadest sense, sex and gender roles, aggression, and belonging or exclusion (with possible reverberations of sibling or oedipal rivalries)—to name just a few. Now the interaction becomes infinitely more complex as it is experienced through each participant's subjectivity, depending to some degree on the conscious and unconscious salience of the interaction for each of them and how are they perceiving the other's response in turn. Thus, each mothering interaction alluded to illustratively above entails an elaborate dynamic field, the key parameters of which, when repeated in a consistent and continuous fashion, are internalized and symbolically represented.

## maternal functions

If we borrow for a moment Bowlby's notion of an internal working model and think of how repeated interactions around what I would like to call maternal functions are experienced—that is, how lived moments *with* a mothering one (which would have to include her absence when needed) are experienced through one's subjectivity, stored as memory, and encoded as representations—then we are approaching the way in which I think it is most fruitful to conceptualize maternal representation (Lichtenberg, 1983; Stern, 1989). To elaborate, I offer three categories of maternal functions that are necessary, if not sufficient, for optimal psychological growth.

1. Security functions. These provide sustenance, comfort, protection, and soothing from actual and potential harm, as well as from perceived psychological threat.

2. Regulatory functions. These have to do with the modulation of affect and stimulation. Through "good enough mothering," which includes both management of the environment and attunement to the child's changing needs, the mothering one facilitates the child's efforts to both contain and appropriately respond to a range of desires; sexual and aggressive feelings; stress and frustration; activity, excitement, and joy; sadness, loss, and yearning. In the realm of stimulation I include the modulation, and provision when necessary, of affective, cognitive, and kinesthetic stimuli.

3. Functions of recognition. I am in agreement with Benjamin (1988), that "recognition is that response from the other which makes meaningful the feelings, intentions, and action of the self" (p. 12). Central to the development of true self-in-relation, according to the intersubjective view, it is through the earliest recognition of one's feelings and behavior by an other that the self becomes real. In earliest infancy this occurs as some form of mutual attunement, but later, as a child is capable of more complex behaviors coupled with greater intentionality and is capable of realizing the subjectivity of the other, the mutual dance of recognition becomes ever more subtle, requiring multilayered, multiconscious tuning.

## from mothers to mothering ones

It has been both my theoretical contention and my clinical observation that we need to revise our assumptions about mothers, about who and what they are. Some examples:

Two lesbians raise a girl adopted at birth. They separate when she is four. The legal adoptive mother retains custody and the co-parent has visitation two nights per week, alternate weekends, and two weeks during the summer—a fairly standard custody arrangement. The coparent has a new lover with whom she shares parenting on visitations. There is no contact with the birth mother.

In a working-class family with one son, the father holds a variety of blue-collar jobs, the mother works as a nurse on the 4 P.M. to midnight shift. When the child is a preschooler, mother works during the day and father works nights. As he comes of school age, their shifts change so that in each case he is primarily in the care of his father. In this family, father is felt to be the *real* mother by the son.

In a single-parent family, a heterosexually identified mother adopts a female child at birth. The mother works and the child spends a significant portion of time with a female child-care worker who lives in the home.

Who is the mother in these families, and what does that mean? Granted, the families are atypical, but not radically so given that most parents work and that paid child care or child care by extended family members is increasingly a reality even for infants, and given the growing numbers of single-parent and blended families. Many, many children today have a number of people in their lives who nurture and care for them and with whom they have consistent and repeated interactions in a form that they will internalize as maternal representations.

Bowlby recognized that attachment needs extend to a small number of familiar people who are in close, consistent proximity to a child. Research has demonstrated that there is no necessary concordance between the attachment styles to mothers and fathers (Bretherton &

Waters, 1985). The same might be said for unconscious representations of maternal figures, the actual mothering ones in a child's life: two coparents in a lesbian household, a grandparent, a child-care worker, a mothering father.

In designating mothering ones, I am making a distinction similar to Ruddick (1989) in differentiating birthing labor, which only women do, from the performance of what I call maternal functions, which women usually do, but not necessarily. Young children will internalize and represent their relationships with these mothering ones as they perform maternal functions, and it is these representations of internalized relations that I thus refer to as maternal representations.

## in sum

The de-construction of gendered motherhood allow us to envisage a new parenting subject that would be less unitary and more conditional, a conception of mothering that transcends gender. It is an active identity, existing within a temporal frame. Moreover, by this construct, mothering is viewed as a relational activity and the mothering/infant dyad as one where mutual subjectivity is implicit.

How then are we to think about maternal representations? A pattern of repeated and consistent lived moments with a mothering one (which would have to include her absence when needed) is experienced through one's subjectivity, stored as memory, and encoded first kinesthetically or proprioceptively and then symbolically as representations. Maternal functions, specifically functions of security, regulation, and recognition, are central to the mothering relation. The ways in which maternal functions are both manifest and subjectively experienced within mothering-child interactions—so as to be internalized and represented unconsciously as one aspect of self and other in relation—are key in the construction of maternal representations.

Security functions provide sustenance, comfort, protection, and soothing from actual and potential harm as well as from perceived psychological threat. The nature of the internalizations of this aspect of mothering relations reflects on a child's ability to grow into a self-sufficient, self-caring, and nurturant adult. Regulatory functions, having to do with the modulation of affect and stimulation, have a variegated effect on character style, modes of learning, and defensive operations. Functions of recognition serve to validate and give meaning to the budding sense of self. Disturbances or dysfunctions in this area of mothering relations have serious consequences for the development of healthy narcissism and consequently for all aspects of relatedness.

Whereas developmentalists might be more interested in the objectively observable manifest interactions between mothering ones and children, psychoanalysts need to deal both theoretically and clinically with the subjective experience of these interactions.

What are the roles of fantasy and defensive operations in the memory and encoding of the lived interactions with the mothering one? How might these manifest themselves in transferential enactments within an analytic setting? How do the unconscious maternal representations of the analyst affect the lived moments with the analysand, and are they as equally accessible within the analysis?

These and many other complex questions arise as we shift our conception of maternal representations from a more or less unitary object incorporated or introjected in the service of preservation or repression, to a varied, symbolically encoded series of relations between two subjects, one of whom is performing maternal functions.

The reconstruction of motherhood implies the reconstruction of families as well.[14] Mothering no longer rests within the confines of of a heterosexual matrix, nor is it bounded by a gender/binaried foundation.

## notes

1. Quoted in the *New York Times*, August 13, 1990.

2. Essentialism most generally can be said to refer to those theories of sexual difference that are primarily biologically determined and that look to discover, define, and describe innate and intrinsic elements of the masculine

and the feminine. Social constructionists look to culture, and the language and ideology embedded therein, as historically determined creators of gender and gender role.

3. According to Singer & Deschamps (1994) there are currently between one and five million lesbian mothers in the United States and between six and fourteen million children who have lesbian or gay parents (pp. 36-37).

4. For Mary Whitehead-Gould's version of the events, see Whitehead with Schwartz-Nobel (1989).

5. For a good introduction to the evolution of relational theory see Mitchell (1988).

6. Sheldon Roth's (1988) is one exception. He views the "negative oedipal" in girls as a normative phase, important to the development of a sense of subjective sexuality. His notion, however, is embedded in his assumption of a healthy heterosexual outcome.

7. Despite inroads in the state's hegemony of heterosexuality and families, as of 1994, only 6 states permit adoption by same-sex couples. Most adoptions by gay or lesbian couples are officially recorded as single parent adoptions. (Singer & Deschamps 1994).

8. Elizabeth Kane (a pseudonym) has published book about her experience entitled *Birth Mother: America's First Legal Surrogate Mother, Her Change of Heart.*

9. In later work (Chodorow, 1994) questions the psychoanalytic understanding of "normative" heterosexuality, that is, the basis for the psychoanalytic premise that the development of heterosexuality is normative.

10. Winnicott's (1956) essay on "Primary Maternal Preoccupation," pp. 300-305, notwithstanding.

11. In keeping with my concept of mothering as an active relation capable of being performed by a variety of caretaking persons in specific relationships to a child, I refer to "mothering ones" whereas Beebe refers to "mothers" in the more traditional sense.

12. Although we are discussing the internalization of experience at an early age, it is not at all certain that representation occurs during the first year. Lichtenberg (1983) argued that it is not until the second year that a growing child develops the capacity to represent self and others at a conceptual level.

13. Ainsworth (1979) and her followers have done some of the most fertile research on attachment behavior, focusing on what they term secure, avoidant, and ambivalent non-pathological styles of attachment.

14. For an extensive discussion of a new family discourse, see K. Weston (1991) *Families We Choose: Lesbians, Gays, Kinship.* New York: Columbia University Press.

# coming out/being heard*

a coming out story would be
a chronicle of all the days of all my lives
it seems there is either nothing to tell,
     or far too much
how can i possibly capture any of it
stop the flow
march it out in lines for all to see and know
i am always coming out
endlessly unfolding on an infinite number of levels
i struggle and persist

           —CONSTANCE FAYE, *Come Again*

*A version of this paper was delivered at the Spring Meeting of the Psychoanalytic Division 39 of the American Psychological Association in New York City, April 1996.

As clinicians, we must be aware that the lesbian community in this country is very diverse racially, ethnically, and culturally. Not only are there Native American, Euro-American, African American, Latina, Asian American lesbians, but there are also lunar dykes (spiritually oriented), granola dykes ('60s' culture), femmes into high heels, make-up, and designer fashion, and lesbians who eschew those very accouterments of traditional femininity. There are lesbians openly engaged in sadomasochistic sexual practices (Samois, 1981), women who choose to live in long, emotionally monogamous relationships with women who would never identify with the lesbian community (Brown, 1993), and women who are self-identified as lesbians living in partnered but largely asexual relationships (Rothblum, 1994). And there are abled and differently abled, older and younger lesbians, who often struggle to understand each other's experience.

It might seem like a contradiction in terms—no, more of a rip tide working against the postmodern current—to write about clinical issues in working with lesbians, as if "lesbians" were a meaningful, unitary, clinical category. One might well ask if we want to talk this way and is it meaningful to do so (Grimshaw, 1986; Bordo, 1990). What are the parameters of the category "lesbian" for clinical work? Is a woman defined as a lesbian by her behavior, her homoerotic fantasies, her identification with the lesbian community, or some combination of the above? Is being a lesbian a singular identification, or secondary to an identification of race, class, or ethnicity?

For purposes of this circumscribed discussion, the term *lesbian* will refer to what Burch (1993) has designated "primary lesbians,"—that is, women whose sexual and emotional bonds are primarily with women, who acknowledge them as such, and who choose to identify with the category. Meeting this definition of lesbian requires a kind of *coming out*, that is, the acknowledgment to self and others that it is primarily women who are desired to meet emotional and erotic needs.

Women often seek psychoanalysis/psychotherapy consciously or unconsciously in order to facilitate this coming out process, hoping (fearing) that the therapeutic work will reveal (hide) a truer self that may find expression in a supportive holding environment. And with the elaboration of the multiplicity of sexual selves comes the fear (hope) that they are really straight (because of the possible existence or perhaps persistence of their heterosexual eroticism). And then there are the worries that their "not a real girlhood" might come out which might be a relief if it did not leave them in the fantasized limbo of the third sex, which in a binary sexed society is like having no sex at all and, hence, being no one at all.

The first section of this chapter will address the ways in which coming out may facilitate the unveiling of more authentic feeling self-states (Winnicott, 1960) yet also serve as another form of masquerade. Closeted sexuality is but one manifestation of false self-states that develop in an environment hostile to the growth of spontaneous subjective desire.

The second section of the chapter will address countertransference issues that arise in the analyst's ability to hear and recognize the lesbian's struggle to come out.

## coming out

A search of the psychoanalytic literature from 1976 through 1997 reveals only one article written solely or partially about coming out (Magee & Miller, 1994). At first, it would seem a bit of a conundrum that a phenomenon so controversial within the culture (mainstream and homosexually identified) has no representation within psychoanalysis.[1] Given that until 1973 homosexuality was equated with pathology by the official psychiatric establishment (Flaks, 1992), and that it remains that way for vocal members of the psychoanalytic establishment (Socarides, 1978; Siegel, 1988; Nicolosi, 1991), it becomes less surprising that *coming out*, a gay-affirmative phrase signifying a complex process of identity formation, would not be recognized by the psychoanalytic community. Moreover, it was not until the early part of this decade that gay- and lesbian-identified psychoanalysts were openly accepted within psychoanalytic training institutes.[2] Their coming out has only just begun, and with it has come a critique of the homophobia within the theory and practice of psychoanalysis (Blechner, 1993; O'Connor & Ryan, 1993; Frommer, 1994; Domenici & Lesser, 1995).

Coming out issues often involve the painful reliving of conflicts with family, the loss of heterosexual privilege, and the conflation of sexual orientation with issues of gender—all appropriate grist for the psychoanalytic mill. Growing up homosexual in America requires sorting through, in some psychic fashion, those nuances of gender and sexuality just now being articulated by our current gender and queer theorists. It can be quite a burden for an individual adult, and even more overwhelming for a child or adolescent.

There have been a few recent efforts to address the ways in which the psychoanalytic community has misheard, misunderstood, and misperceived women, lesbians, and their sexuality (Magee & Miller, 1992; O'Connor & Ryan, 1993). Those "misses" in understanding can and have seriously de-railed many a woman's coming out. A few quiet voices within psychoanalysis have cautioned against the overt and veiled attempts to change, convert, deny, or otherwise interpret away homosexual preference, but these have been largely ignored within the psychoanalytic community until quite recently (Mitchell, 1981; Blechner 1993; Corbett, 1993; Frommer, 1994). Many lesbians experience in childhood the inability to name a constellation of feelings seemingly so different from their peers. This leads to later experiences of alienation and emotional isolation, felt most acutely during adolescence and early adulthood. But for some, the "closeting" of homoerotic feelings comprises only a further layering of a false self-structure whose foundation lies in infancy with primary caretaking others.

Struggling to find the language to represent that which they cannot be, many lesbians in treatment, when speaking about their sense of gendered self, tend to describe themselves in the "not" voice rather than in a positive declarative form. "Not a regular girl." "Not at all like my mother or sisters." "Not a real girl." They are what they are not rather than what they are; for refusing to accept what is perceived to be their femininity, they have foreclosed an affirmative sense of gender. In earlier work, I have written about the sense of "not being a real girl" in terms of the *girlness*, that is, of being not female like mother (A. Schwartz, 1986, 1988ab, 1994).[3] However, in this instance, not being a real girl, being a *not real* girl—speaks directly to the experience of inauthenticity. The multiple internalizations of pseudo-compliant interactions with significant others masks one's true self's impulses toward subjectivity and the flowering of desire until they are so well hidden that they threaten to disappear.

Coming out, then, is about feeling *real*. Coming out is about maximizing the ability to experience and express authentic desire, intimacy, and subjectivity in whatever form that might take.

For lesbians, gender is often the first arena in which the representation of truer self/false self conflicts becomes conscious. Many lesbians seem to have been precocious in their sensitivity to asymmetries of gender privilege, both in the home and in the culture at large. They are bothered by the pervasive feeling, usually unarticulated to themselves or others, that there is "something wrong." Fantasies, which during childhood may seem to include the wish to be a boy, upon further inquiry devolve into wishes to have the *adventures, experiences, or privileges* that boys have. The cultural mode for activity, mastery, and excitement has, until quite recently, been almost exclusively male. The wish is for the symbolic phallus, not the penis. Fantasies based on these wishes, incorporating a heightened sense of empowerment, can be, and are often, masculine in form. The clitoris finds little representation in the unconscious language of dreams (Kulish, 1991).

The interpersonal predicament becomes how to share this world with other children: the chafing at social constraints, the refusal to accept one's prescribed and restricted gender role. To make the point concretely: Which childhood girlfriend's tea party should my patient (growing up in the 1960s, when the second wave of feminism was still nascent) attend when she, in her fantasies, was the King of Jordan?

A feeling of difference from peers in childhood is exacerbated during pre- and early adolescence when young lesbians find themselves truly not interested in the "boy talk" of their friends. Although they might have boyfriends themselves, their desire is more often sparked by a mysterious attraction, a yearning for a female teacher, camp counselor, another girl friend. How to talk about it? Best not. Best not to acknowledge those differences. Best not to think about it. Best not to think about me.

However, it is when other aspects of truer self-in-relation—one's curiosities and wonder, angers and loves, jealousies, anxieties, and doubts, the emotional stuff of which we are all made—become associated in some way with sexuality and gender that the issues become complex and confusing. Thus it happens—to the dismay of some (a dismay that often precipitates entrance into analysis)—that after the first elation of liberation, coming out as a lesbian does not relieve essential feelings of isolation, depression, or emptiness.

For those women seeking treatment whose isolation really is consequent to their sexuality, gaining a knowledge of the extent and heterogeneity of the lesbian community as it exists in many areas of the country, therapeutic support in dealing with family and/or work environments, as well as an exploration of the roots and facets of internalized homophobia, will often suffice in the facilitation of "coming out."

## the analytic issue

The more complex analytic issues arise for those women whose childhoods were filled with a myriad of unacceptable thoughts, impulses, feelings, and object ties, so that lesbian sexuality in its secrecy merely augments and intensifies the already established imperative to hide. Closeted lesbian sexuality does not constitute a false self state, but internalized homophobia may be complicitous to its existence.

According to Winnicott (1960) the growth of a false self occurs when, in earliest infancy, the mothering one fails to meet adequately the infant's spontaneous gesture, impulse, or sensory hallucination (p. 145). It is this nonsynchronous, nonempathic relating that results in the defensive false self, a shielding or hiding behind a mask which prohibits the development of true spontaneity. According to Winnicott, the function of the false self is to "hide and protect the True Self" (1960, p. 142).

Winnicott elucidates a range of false self organizations: At the negative extreme, True Self is totally hidden; in less extreme situations the True Self is acknowledged as a potential and allowed a secret life; here the goal is the preservation of the individual despite a hostile or not "good-enough" environment. The False Self has as its main concern a search for conditions that will make it possible for the True Self to come into its own. If conditions cannot be found, Winnicott suggests, then there must be reorganized a new defense against exploitation of the True Self. If this is not possible, then the clinical result may be suicide. Suicide in this context is the destruction of the total self in avoidance of annihilation of the True Self (p. 143). It is interesting to note in this context that compared to their heterosexual peers, lesbian and gay youths are two to three times more likely to attempt suicide, accounting for up to 30 percent of all completed suicides among youths.[4]

Although Winnicott certainly locates the etiology of False Self within the world of first object relationships, he does not forget about Eros. Winnicott states clearly that the "fusion of the motility and erotic elements is in process of becoming a fact at this period of development" (1960, p. 145). Thus one could say that the infant's first spontaneous gestures would include the first expressions of *desire*.

Bollas (1989) likens the True Self to Lacan's *jouissance* (Lacan, 1960). He defines it as the "subject's inalienable right to ecstasy, a virtually legal imperative to pursue desire" (p. 19–20). Thus, whether one thinks of one's True Self as a function of inherited potential, spontaneous action, a collection of details of the experience of aliveness (Winnicott, 1960, p. 148), or contextually based feelings of authenticity (Mitchell 1963, p. 131), it is based in desire and finds expression through experience that is constructed in an object world.

To return to Winnicott, he reiterates:

> Only the True Self [and we may amend here, true self *experiences*] can be creative and only the True Self [states] can feel real. . . . [T]he existence of a False Self results in feelings of unreality or a sense of futility. When the infant gets seduced into compliance, False Self builds up false sets of relationships and by means of introjections even attains a show of being real. And so we see greater or lesser degrees of compliance and imitation. (1960, p. 147)

True Self *experiences* and True Self *states* more accurately describe the multiplicity of experiences, transcending locatedness, which comprise subjectivity. Mitchell (1992, 1993) prefers to speak of feelings of authenticity and talks of a temporal rather than spatial self. It has no core but rather is comprised of a series of embodied experiences whose meanings are generated through interaction in the object world.

## for lesbians

A dynamic often has been reported in families of lesbians that is similar to that noted by Richard Isay (1989), in his work with gay men and their fathers. The mother retreats from the intensity of their daughter's attachment. Mother's behavior can be profoundly distancing so that the actual and perceived maternal rejection is internalized as a repetitive series of "bad mes" in relation to mother. Such mothers tend to communicate to their daughters, "You are not like me," "You are different and somehow apart." False Self states emerge in the effort to be like and hence to please Mother.

Eisenbud (1982) named a mother's withholding of the possibility of identification with her as one path to lesbian choice, although in Eisenbud's instance the dynamic was one of the mother's narcissistic competitiveness rather than the intensity of the daughter's desire. Clearly the two are not mutually exclusive. Moreover, it is not merely the intensity but the effort of the young girl to be the *agent of desire* in relation to the mother—rather than solely the object of father's desire— that mothers may find threatening.[5]

In their search for agency, toddler girls often turn to their fathers as they experience maternal rejection or distancing or in the natural course of seeking identificatory love. Benjamin (1988) lays out the dilemma for these girls within the context of current gender arrangements: "The girl's wish to identify with her father, even if satisfied, leads to myriad problems under the present gender system. As long as the mother is not articulated as a sexual agent, identification with the father's agency and desire will appear fraudulent and stolen; furthermore it conflicts with the cultural image of woman as sexual object and with the girl's maternal identification. It will not jibe with what she knows about her position in her father's eyes" (p. 111).

Coming out as a lesbian may have to do with sexuality, as it does in many cases, but sexuality can act as a screen in treatment for more complex problems that lie elsewhere. Patients who remain "closeted" are often those with unresolved narcissistic issues, tenuous object relations, whose True Selves are hidden and protected in a swath of shameful lesbian sexuality. Analysis of sexuality in many lesbians revolves not around object choice per se, but around confusions and conflations of sexual orientation and internalized gender identificaions.

Winnicott (1960) cites a case "of a middle aged woman who had a very successful False Self but who had the feeling that all her life she had not started to exist, and that she had always been looking for a means of getting to her True Self" (p. 142). After a long analysis, "she finally came *to the beginning of her life*. She contains no true experience, she has no past. She starts with fifty years of wasted life, but at last she feels real, and therefore she now wants to live" (p. 148). This closely parallels the experience of many patients when coming out to themselves in treatment—even if they have been living openly as lesbians for many years.

They are reclaiming and redefining their gender within the context of their subjectivity. Their womanhood is no longer inimical to agency; their desire, ambition, assertiveness, competitiveness, aggression needn't be defined as male. Coming out as a lesbian is but a special case of the "coming out" of many of our patients. It is the painful unveiling of masquerades (Riviere, 1929) that, through proper use of the analyst, allows the unfolding of more authentic feeling experiences and erotic selves that contain within them the earliest sparks of subjectivity and agency.

## clinical anecdote

Zoe's experiences might illustrate some of the clinical manifestations of the shedding of False Self within analysis. Zoe entered analysis in her mid-twenties, depressed after the break-up of a short relationship with a lover. Although voicing a rhetoric of lesbian feminism, she suffered from an admittedly intense homophobia and envy of heterosexual privilege. She brought in recurrent dreams of where she or other representative lesbians were damaged or in some way mutant with deformed or marred body parts.

Zoe had a long history of hypochondria (stemming from childhood), which ebbed and flowed throughout the early part of the analytic work. The fears usually included some form of chronic and/or fatal illness, later transforming into an obsessive fear of contracting AIDS. Zoe's behavior and dream life seemed to point in the direction of the futility of which Winnicott spoke. She felt doomed to die from AIDS, a fear that represented both her feelings of the ultimate illegitimacy of her lesbianism and helplessness in the face of male aggression. Most of Zoe's fears centered on being penetrated by a sharp, contaminated object. In her sexual behavior, Zoe refused oral sex as not being safe, despite the fact that she and her partner had been tested for AIDS and remained monogamous. These feelings preceded each new move into a flowering of truer self experiences.

Zoe was born into a family with a narcissistically competitive mother and an emotionally/physically abusive and sexually inappropriate father. A graduate of one of the finest universities in the country, Zoe wore her mother's hand-me-downs, and when she entered treatment she had no idea what size clothes or shoes she wore.

Voices have been very important to Zoe. For many months she was enraged at her lover for "changing her voice." She couldn't stand her lover's baby voice or baby talk when they made love. "Why can't she just have one voice for all occasions? Why can't she be the same person all the time? Why does she have to be different with different people? I want a woman who is strong and self-confident, not someone who hides behind being a baby." Of course, Zoe's concerns were largely projective. Months later, Zoe was being driven to distraction by an almost compulsive attention to her own voice. She complained that she was always listening to her voice and that most times she couldn't recognize herself. "It doesn't sound like me. But what is the real me? I don't know."

Zoe had been aware of the ways in which she could act coquettishly in the service of dealing with difficult men she might interact with in her professional life, but at first that had seemed to be a gender performance she enjoyed. However, as she became aware of her father's ongoing emotional abusiveness and lack of appropriate sexual boundaries, the gender performance felt less voluntary and more self-preserving.

Similarly, as Zoe began to dissolve her idealization of her current lover as earth mother and saint, Zoe was distressed at feeling herself "popping out of my body, listening to my own voice, losing my identity." These derealization and depersonalization experiences, which she associated with "going insane," could be viewed as the consequences of the enormous anxiety generated by Zoe's shedding of her inauthentic False Self behavior in relation to the power figures in her life. The persona of a young, confused girl who posed a threat to no one—which she had cultivated since childhood—no longer fit.

As she confronted her history of paternal abuse, she also confronted the sabotaging of her subjectivity in the service of not competing with a failed, occasionally sadistic, and narcissistically vulnerable father, with whom she had seemed to have a very close relationship. This sabotage had successfully paralyzed the forward movement of a very promising but stagnant career, as she was loathe to challenge not only this internal father but also his many collegial representatives in her professional field.

Nothing felt comfortable. Every behavior seemed false as Zoe examined her "butch/femme" roles and the way she used them. She was falsely "femme" with certain key heterosexual men in order to defend herself against imagined consequences of her ambition and competition, and butch with her female lover to defend against her real vulnerability and fears of abandonment.

The discovery and ultimate abandonment of the "not me" personas, which was how Zoe experienced her analysis, left her in terror of finding no "me" at all. Death or insanity seemed preferable, the last bastion of defense against the annihilation of true self (Winnicott, 1960).

For this lesbian, "coming out" included an acknowledgment of the depths of her homophobia, which itself masked an internalization of mother's earliest narcissistically based rejection of her as a possible female competitor. Zoe's analysis opened an arena for the re-examination of gender performance in the constricted stereotypic butch/femme form, and illuminated the ways in which she used her "voice" to reinforce constructed personas at the cost of more agentic, truer self experiences.

## being heard

As lesbians embody the analytic struggle to come out and tell their stories as analysands, the question arises, "Is anyone really listening?" A second clinical anecdote, reconstructed with the responses of two hypothetical analysts, highlights certain issues of countertransference in working with lesbians and bisexual women in treatment.

Yolanda, a professional Euro-American lesbian in her late thirties, begins her analysis. As part of her presenting problems, she haltingly tells of disturbing sexual fantasies in which she is physically overpowered by a male and forced to have intercourse. She feels afraid and psychologically violated. Nevertheless, the fantasy is extremely arousing and, in fact, intrudes upon her lovemaking with her female lover of ten years standing. Sometimes this fantasy seems the only road to orgasm. She feels ashamed of the fantasy and wants it to "just go away." The patient is reluctant to talk about it; she fears that the dream may mean that "she is not *really* a lesbian" and that her life as she knows it is ruined. Yolanda lives with a women whom she loves and with whom she hopes to have children, but their relationship is marred by the patient's recurrent depressions and inability to settle on a career with some satisfaction.

Analyst A responds to the strains of masochism in the patient's fantasy or, as she might prefer to express it, to the patient's inability to *directly claim her desire as an active subject*. Sexual orientation is largely irrelevant; she will listen for sado-masochistic dynamics in the analysand's internal object world and correspondingly with significant caretaking figures. Analyst A has treated many women with such fantasies and views them as disorders of desire/agency.

Analyst B counters, but can one ignore the heterosexual context? What do we make of that, and to the patient's worry that maybe she's not *really* a lesbian? Analyst B wonders if perhaps this feminine looking young woman isn't a lesbian after all. Perhaps the intractability of her depression is a result of her inability to adequately separate from the maternal and move on to a truly differentiated genital stage of development. Perhaps her homosexual involvements are primarily pre-oedipal and thus ultimately unsatisfying, especially for someone who claims so badly to want a child. A good analysis might spare her the pain of living a marginalized, deviant life style.

Is this divergence in the responses to Yolanda's fantasy a matter of divergence in theoretical orientation, as it might appear, or primarily a function of countertransference? Is it meaningful to differentiate the two, given the decentering of psychoanalytic truth and the eclipse of the universality of normative psychosexual development? Clearly, a postmodern perspective on psychoanalytic process would suggest not. But even before such critiques entered the discourse, the distinction began to blur. Levenson (1974), an early and vocal proponent of the Interpersonal School, maintained that "all psychodynamic interpretations, just as all metapsychologies, become, in the end, acts of countertransference" (p. 365). Similarly, Kwawer (1980) points out, in one of the few psychoanalytic papers on countertransference in clinical work with homosexuals, that how the therapist thinks, talks, and chooses to interpret issues about and around homosexuality are all a function of the therapist's countertransference (p. 73).

In Yolanda's case, in accordance with Analyst A, issues of dominance/submission played a large part in the analysis of both the paternal and maternal transference and were seen to be integrally woven in her narcissistic issues as well. As these issues were analyzed and worked through, the heterosexual fantasies so prevalent early in the analysis largely disappeared and no longer intruded upon lovemaking. Not surprisingly, as Yolanda was able to mourn the premature death of her father, more conscious heterosexual desires surfaced. These were much more easily integrated into Yolanda's sense of her sexuality as one of the many roads not traveled as a consequence of making a lifelong monogamous commitment to a lover and life partner.

How might the analysis have proceeded had Yolanda been working with Analyst B? Might this be one of those analyses where countless years would have been wasted trying to convince the analysand that her completed analysis will result in a fulfilling heterosexuality (Blechner, 1993)? Might Analyst B be suffering from heterophilia, which D. Schwartz (1993) defined as the "overvaluing of intimate relations between different-sexed partners" (p. 643), so that the analyst, often unwittingly, takes for granted the psychological desirability of "vaginal heterosexual intercourse, reproduction, marriage" (p. 651)?

Critics of traditional psychoanalytic practice have suggested that both conscious and unconscious biases against the desirability of a homosexual outcome affect the course of treatment (Blechner, 1993; D. Schwartz, 1993; Frommer, 1994). One might attempt to counsel "technical neutrality" in the face of a life-style choice of object or gender performance, as Mitchell does (1981). The problem then becomes determining upon what ground is that so-called neutrality based, and whether claims to "neutrality" mask countertransferential homophobic reactions that are difficult for the analyst to acknowledge or deal with.

A footnote in Freud's classic case of Dora (1905) points to his countertransferential blunders:

> The longer the interval of time that separates me from the end of this analysis, the more probable it seems to me that the fault in my technique lay in this omission: I failed to discover in time and to inform the patient that her homosexual (gynaecophilic) love for Frau K. was the strongest unconscious current in her mental life. . . . Before I had

learnt the importance of the homosexual current of feeling in psy-
choneurotics, I was often brought to a standstill in the treatment of
my cases or found myself in compete perplexity. (p. 143)

If we look to more recently published clinical data about psychoanalytic work with lesbians, we see very little in the way of guideposts with
which to wend our way through the miasma of theory or technique
(Deutsch, 1933; Siegel, 1988; Irigaray, 1991). In an extensive review of
the psychoanalytic literature on homosexuality, Kwawer (1980) found
much speculation about the etiology, genetics, and dynamics of homosexuality and almost nothing about actually *treating* homosexuals, by
which he implicitly meant men. He notes, almost as an afterthought,
that the literature is "largely silent on the question of treating homosexuality in women" (p. 78). The invisibility of homosexuality in the
clinical literature as a focus of transference/countertransference exami-
nation remained, with few exceptions, throughout the following
decade.

What this means, of course, is that not only is there precious little
written by lesbians about lesbians but also that within the tradition of
psychoanalytic training itself, a lesbian's experience can be severely
truncated. How can a personal training analysis proceed when one's
sexuality is suspect? How can a lesbian trainee adequately present
countertransference issues to a clinical supervisor who might view
strains of that countertransference as signs of pathology or "arrested
development"?

Not surprisingly, then, most of the reports of clinical work with lesbians in this country come from outside the psychoanalytic walls, for
there has been no safe passageway into the forbidden city. This foreclosure of the sharing of lived variegated sexual experience with the psychoanalytic body has, I believe, profound implications for our work.

As Racker (1968) so clearly stated, the "understanding of transference will depend on the analyst's capacity to identify himself both with

the analysand's impulses and defenses, and with his internal objects, and to be conscious of these identifications. This ability in the analyst will in turn depend upon the degree to which he accepts his countertransference, for his countertransference is likewise based on identification with the patient's id and ego and his internal objects" (p. 131).

Heterophilia, internalized homophobia, and/or the dissociation of one's own homosexual desires will preclude these experiences. More explicit transgressions of gender norms, radical representations of butch/femme, and transgendered persons are often threatening in a culture where gender roles exist as a basic cognitive organizer (Kohlberg, 1966). For instance, Siegel (1988) argues theoretically for a universal pathology of lesbian sexuality as a function of severe maternal deficits coupled with an alleged lack of internal representation of a vagina. When she then writes about how her lesbian patient's oral aggressive fantasies made her nauseous, a countertransference feeling that she attributes solely to *induced* feelings of hurt and rage, one may well wonder whether Siegel has accurately considered the sources of her countertransferential malaise.

For female clinicians, lesbian eroticism may become difficult in a number of ways. Many heterosexual women are unaccustomed to being the object of female desire and feel uncomfortable with it. Clinicians are liable to turn a deaf ear to the re-emergence of formerly disavowed erotic longings for mother and other maternal caretakers as well as to the rekindling of the homoerotic desire that exists within unconsummated pre-adolescent, adolescent, or more mature friendships.

McDougall (1986) writes quite eloquently about just such "countertransference deafness." In a very interesting case of a presumably heterosexually identified woman, McDougall points to her countertransference as the key to the stalled analyses of her female patient. A dream of her own awakens McDougall to her countertransference resistance to acknowledging her envy of her patient's allegedly possessive mother. McDougall carefully examines her "need to keep in repression my own childlike wish to be the chosen subject of her mother's erotic desire" and thus only belatedly is able to recognize her patient's desire to have a homosexually desirous mother (p. 226).

This "countertransference deafness" also narrowed McDougall's understanding of her patient's phobic anxieties and related intruder fantasies, which had been interpreted solely as the patient's perception of heterosexual sex as violent. Throughout a good portion of the analysis, there had been no mention of women in the patient's daydreams. Once "permission" was granted by the analyst for the analysand to experience erotic fantasies having to do with mother, their entire nature changed. "It is sufficient to say that the window-intruder was of a thoroughly *bisexual* nature. My countertransference deafness had been an opaque screen, hiding not only the analytic exploration of Madame T's erotic fantasies, but also further insight into their underlying significance, especially in their homosexual dimension" (1986, p. 227).

The conflation of theory and transference/countertransference interpretation plagues clinicians throughout their work, but it is especially germane in conceptualizing issues of gender and sexuality. Often, as is the case in Siegel's work (1988), the sexualized homosexual transferences that develop are viewed as pre-oedipal—a defense against deep early longings for the "unavailable" mother—rather than as the oedipal/genital transferences that they might be. Thus lesbian sexuality gets pushed down the developmental slide toward domains of arrest, deficit, and infantile sexuality. And, as we have seen, such fixed paradigms can obscure the vision of the analyst to other paradigms in the transference (Kulish, 1986).

Sheldon Roth (1988), in arguing for the recognition of the negative oedipal phase (that is, the rivalry of the little girl with her father for the love of the mother) in all women, points out that "for the male analyst, when homosexual issues emerge, the technical stumbling block is the reductive trap of oversimplifying the complexity of female sexuality into an either/or conceptualization; the analysand is either longing for dyadic fusion (yearning for the maternal breast) or fleeing from the anxieties of positive oedipal sexuality. However, homosexual issues, deriving from the negative oedipal development, may be paramount in and of themselves" (p. 35–36).

Many lesbians have a history of sexual relationships with men. They have had friends with whom they have had sex, boyfriends with whom they have had relationships, husbands with whom they have shared portions of their lives and raised children. Care must be taken not to collude with the pseudo-compliant and/or homophobic defenses of the lesbian patient to interpret heteroerotic desires as the truer expression of self (emphasizing the gender of the object over the nature of the object tie) and the homoerotic as the defensive/arrested/compensatory/regressed compromise. It may be particularly difficult for a male clinician to see, at first, that flirtatious behavior and erotic heterosexual fantasies—including transferential ones about the analyst—might be defensive as well, as it was with the patient of one supervisee, a way of warding off the threat of male aggression, a part of the female masquerade (Riviere, 1929).

Roth (1988) sees the triangular rivalry for the mother to be an important step in the development of girls, as it is an active phase of emerging sexuality and not primarily a regression from the oedipal situation. We might say that the rivalry with a caretaking other, for mother, affords an opportunity for the little girl to experience herself as sexual subject, and that in turn is requisite for a healthy sense of one's womanhood. Thus Roth recognizes the daughter's longings as having a truly erotic rather than solely maternal component, and he recognizes this eroticism as being integral to a young girl's developing sense of competence and agency in the world.

Roth's theoretical qualification, however, is embedded in a normative, developmental model of heterosexuality. The "negative oedipal" phase as conceived of by Roth is one poised between the "pre-oedipal" and truly "genital" on a girl's relentless march toward heterosexuality. However, he does lay the groundwork for a (homo)sexuality in woman that is built on a sense of agency rather than defeat, where erotic desires are recognized as such, rather than made invisible in a swamp of pre-oedipal undergrowth.

## a word

A word to those lesbian-identified therapists and analysts, who are "out" either to individual patients or to their professional communities, not to err in the opposite direction, that is by overidentification with a fantasied "lesbian" whose sexuality and life issues are somewhat known and understood.

When a lesbian patient asks for a lesbian therapist or analyst, and the appropriate referral is made, there is, in my experience, often a silent pact that the patient proffers as part of the therapeutic contract: *We are lesbians and therefore we have some common understandings that need not be articulated.* This reflects a wish of the patient (or couple) to be understood completely and profoundly, a wish that is not necessarily an indication of narcissistic pathology nor necessarily a manifestation of a regressive wish for symbiotic merger with the mother, but rather often is a reflection of the fear of once again feeling alienated, even with one's own therapist. It is a magical wish to undue the years of isolation, and ultimately a defense against re-experiencing those painful feelings that protect the coming out the of True Self.

The lesbian therapist or analyst may easily collude with such a wish as it possibly taps into her similar experiences and recalls her past or current yearnings to be part of, joined with, an enlivened family or community. The unconscious joining of the patient's current and the therapist's past isolated selves creates a countertransference problem. The traditional analytic or mental health community can be a lonely place for a lesbian clinician, with real sanctions for being "out." Hence, there is the strong temptation to feel "at home" in the consulting room.

As clinicians, regardless of our sexual orientation or that of our patients, we must always walk that fine line between *over-* and *under-*identification with the individuals, couples, and families with whom we work. Overpathologizing problems in living and differences in values and life styles can and does lead to the objectification of patients into the realm of Other, a category that is ultimately unknowable. Yet, the assumption of sameness based on apparent similarities of values and life style can defeat the very goal of the analytic inquiry: namely, the elucidation of the life history and circumstance that has brought the patient into therapy or psychoanalysis; the unique configuration of family dynamics, constitutional predispositions, and life choices that make for our individual membership in the human community.

### notes

1. It is interesting that President Clinton's original inititatve to allow gay men and lesbians to serve in the military was compromised to construct the infamous "Don't ask, don't tell policy", which, in essence, says that the military establishment accepts homosexuality but rejects "coming out."

2. Personal communication from Ronnie Lesser, Ph.D., founding member of the Committee for Gay and Lesbian Concerns at the New York University Postdoctoral Program in Psychotherapy and Psychoanalysis.

3. This is discussed more fully in "a lesbian is . . . a lesbian is not" in this volume.

4. U.S. Department of Health and Human Services, "Report of the Secretary's Task Force on Youth Suicide," 1989, as reported in Singer & Descamps (1994), p.77.

5. Mother's own repressed homosexual desires, as well as a rejection of her object status in relation to men, are disavowed through her distancing of her daughter.

# references

Abelin, E. 1971. The Role of the Father in the Separation-Individuation Process. In *Separation-Individuation*. Ed. by J. B. McDevitt and C. F. Settlage. New York: International Universities Press, pp. 229–252.

———. 1980. Triangulation, the Role of the Father and the Origins of Core Gender Identity During the Rapprochement Subphase. In *Rapprochement*, Ed. by R. F. Lax, S. Bach, & J. A. Burland. New York: Aronson, pp. 151–170.

Abelove, H., Barale, M., & Halperin, D. (Eds.) 1993. *The Lesbian and Gay Studies Reader*. New York: Routledge.

Ainsworth, M. 1979. Attachment as Related to Mother-Infant Interaction. In *Advances in the Study of Behavior*. Ed. by J. B. Rosenblatt, R. A. Hinde, C. Beer, & M. Bushel. New York : Academic, pp. 135–145.

Alonso, A., & Schippers, L. 1986. Object Relations Theory and Mid-Life Development. *Dynamic Psychotherapy* 4(1), 5–10.

Altman, D. 1979. *Coming Out in the Seventies*. Sydney: Wild & Wooley.

Applegarth, A. 1976. Some Observations on Work Inhibition in Women. *Journal of the American Psychoanalytic Association* 24, 251–268.

Aron, L. 1995. The Internalized Primal Scene. *Psychoanalytic Dialogues*, 5(1), 195–237.

Atwood. M. 1987. *The Handmaid's Tale*. New York: Ballantine.

*Bar Girls*, 1994, adapted for screen by Laura Hoffman; director, Marita Giovanni.

Bar On, B-A. 1992. The Feminist Sexuality Debates and the Transformation of the Political. *Hypatia*, 7(4), 45–58.

Baruch, G., Barnett, R., & Rivers, C. 1983. *Lifeprints: New Patterns of Love and Work for Today's Women*. New York: McGraw-Hill.

Bassin, D. 1989. Women's Shifting Sense of Self: The Impact of Reproductive Technology. In *Gender in Transition: A New Frontier*. Ed. by J. Offerman-Zuckerberg. New York: Plenum.

———. 1996. Beyond the He and the She: Toward the Reconciliation of Masculinity and Feminity in the Postoedipal Female Mind. *Journal of the American Psychoanalytic Association*. Special Supplement 4:157–190.

Bassin, D., Honey, M., & Kaplan, M. (Eds.) 1994. *Representations of Motherhood*. New Haven: Yale University Press.

Beebe, B. 1986. Mother-Infant Mutual Influence and Pre-Cursors of Self-Object Representations. In *Empirical Studies of Psychoanalytic Theories*. Vol. 2. Ed. by J. Masling. Hillsdale, NJ: Analytic Press, pp. 27–48.

Benedek, T. 1973. On the Organization of the Reproduction Drive. *Psychoanalytic Investigation: Selected Papers*. New York: Quadrangle/New York Times Book Co. pp. 408–445.

Benjamin, J. 1988. *The Bonds of Love, Psychoanalytic Feminism and the Problem of Domination*. New York: Pantheon.

———. 1995. Sameness and Difference: An Overinclusive View of Gender Constitution. *Psychoanalytic Inquiry, 15*, 125–142.

———. 1996. Gender Ambiguity. *Gender and Psychoanalysis, 1*(1), 27–43.

Benstock, S. 1986. *Women of the Left Bank, Paris, 1900–1940*. Austin: University of Texas Press.

Blechner, M. 1993. Homophobia in Psychoanalytic Writing and Practice. *Psychoanalytic Dialogues*, 3, 627–637.

Blumstein, P. & Schwartz, P. 1983. *American Couples*. New York: William Morrow.

Bollas, C. 1989. *Forces of Destiny: Psychoanalysis and Human Idiom*. Northvale, NJ: Jason Aronson.

Bordo, S. 1990. Feminism, Postmodernism, and Gender-Scepticism. In *Feminism/Postmodernism*. Ed. by L. Nicholson. New York & London: Routledge, pp. 133–156.

Bowlby, J. 1973. *Attachment and Loss: Volume 2. Separation*. New York: Basic Books.

———. 1980. *Attachment and Loss: Volume 3. Loss, Sadness, Depression*. New York: Basic Books.

———. 1988. *A Secure Base: Clinical Applications of Assessment Theory*. London: Routledge.

Brazelton, T. B. 1980. Neonatal Assessment. In *The Course of Life: Psychoanalytic Contributions Toward Understanding Personality Development: Vol. 1. Infancy and Early Childhood*. Ed. by S. I. Greenspan & G. H. Pollock. & Rockville, MD.: NIMH.

Bretherton, I., & Waters, E. (Eds.) 1985. *Growing Points in Attachment Theory and Research. Monographs of the Society for Research in Child Development, 50* (1–2, Serial No. 209), 66–104.

Brown, L. 1993. The Boston Marriage in the Therapy Office. In *Boston Marriages: Romantic but Asexual Relationships Among Contemporay Lesbians*. Ed. by E. Rothblum & K. Brehony. Amherst: University of Massachusetts Press, pp. 86–95.

Burch, B. 1993. *On Intimate Terms: The Psychology of Difference in Lesbian Relationships.* Urbana and Chicago: University of Illinois Press.

Butler, J. 1990a. *Gender Trouble and the Subversion of Identity.* New York & London: Routledge.

———. 1990b. *Gender Trouble, Feminist Theory, and Psychoanalytic Discourse In Feminism/Postmodernism.* Ed. by L. Nicholson. New York & London: Routledge, pp. 324–340.

———. 1991. Imitation and Gender Insubordination. In *Inside/Out: Lesbian Theories, Gay Theories.* Ed. by D. Fuss. New York: Routledge, pp. 13–31. Also in Imitation and Gender Insubordination. In *The Lesbian and Gay Studies Reader.* Ed. by H. Abelove, M. Barale, & D. Halperin. New York: Routledge, pp. 307–320.

———. 1993a. *Bodies That Matter: On the Discursive Limits of Sex.* New York: Routledge.

———. 1993b. The Lesbian Phallus and the Morphological Imaginary. *Bodies That Matter: On the Discursinve Limits of Sex.* New York: Routledge, pp. 57–91.

———. 1995. Melancholy Gender-Refused Identifications. *Psychoanalytic Dialogues,* 5(2); 165–180.

Case, S. 1988–1989. Towards a Butch-Femme Aesthetic. *Discourse, 11* (Winter), 55–73.

Caspar, V., Shultz, S., & Wickens, E. 1992. Breaking the Silences: Lesbian and Gay Parents and the Schools. *Teachers College Record, 94*(1), 109–137.

Chasseguet-Smirgel, J. 1976. The Consideration of Some Blind Spots in the Exploration of the "Dark Continent." *International Journal of Psychoanalysis, 58,* 275–286.

Chessler, P. 1989. *The Sacred Bond: Legacy of Baby M.* New York: Random House.

Chodorow, N. 1978. *The Reproduction of Mothering: Psychoanalysis and the Sociology of Gender.* Berkeley: University of California Press.

———. 1994. *Femininities, Masculinities, Sexualities: Freud and Beyond.* Lexington: University of Kentucky Press.

Cixous, H. 1986. Sorties. *In The Newly Born Woman.* Trans. Betsy Wing. Ed. by Cixous, H. & C. Clement C. Minneapolis: University of Minnesota Press. Originally published as *La Jeune Née.* Paris: Union Generale d'Editions, 1975.

Clausen, J. 1990. My Interesting Condition. *Outlook* (Winter), 10–21.

Coates, S. 1990. Ontogenesis of Boyhood Gender Identity Disorder. *Journal of the American Psychoanalytic Association, 18,* 414–438.

Coates, S., Friedman, R., & Wolfe, S. 1991. The Etiology of Boyhood Gender Disorder: A Model for Integrating Treatment, Development and Psychodynamics. *Psychoanalytic Dialogues, 1*(4), 481–524.

Corbett, K. 1993. The Mystery of Homosexuality. *Psychoanalytic Psychology,*
*10*(3), 349–358.

Cordova, J. 1992. Butch, Lesbians and Feminism. *In The Persistent Desire: A*
*Femme-Butch Reader.* Ed. by J. Nestle. Boston: Alyson, pp.
272–294.

Crawford, S. 1987. *Lesbian Families: Psychosocial Stress and the Family-Building*
*Process.* In Boston Lesbian Psychology Collective (eds) Lesbian Psychologies University of Illinos Press. pp. 195–214.

*The Crying Game,* 1992, writer/director Neil Jordan.

Daly, M. 1978. *Gyn/Ecology: The Metaethics of Radical Feminism.* Boston: Beacon.

Daumer, E. 1992. Queer Ethics, or The Challenge of Bisexuality to Lesbian
Ethics. *Hypatia,* 7(4), 91–106.

de Beauvoir, S. 1952. *The Second Sex.* New York: Bantam.

D'Ercole, A. 1996. Postmodern Ideas About Gender and Sexuality: The Lesbian Woman Redundancy. *Psychoanalysis and Psychotherapy,* *13*(2),
142–152.

De Lauretis, T. 1987. *Technologies of Gender.* Bloomington: Indiana University
Press.

Derrida, J. 1978. *Writing and Difference.* London: Routledge & Kegan Paul.

Deutsch, H. 1925. Psychology of Women's Sexual Functions. *International*
*Journal of Psychoanalysis,* 65, 58–62.

———. 1933. Homosexuality in Women. *International Journal of Psychoanalysis,*
*14,* 34–56.

Dimen, M. 1991. Deconstructing Difference: Gender, Splitting and Transitional Space. *Psychoanalytic Dialogues,* *1*(3), 335–352.

———. 1995. On "Our Nature": Prolegomenon to a Relational Theory of Sexuality. In *Disorienting Sexuality: Psychoanalytic Reappraisals of Sexual*
*Identities.* Ed. by T. Domenici & R. Lesser. New York: Routledge,
pp.1 29–152.

Dinnerstein, D. 1977. *The Mermaid and the Minotaur.* New York: Harper.

Doan, L. (Ed.), 1994. *The Lesbian Postmodern.* New York: Columbia University
Press.

Domenici, T. 1995. Exploding the Myth of Sexual Psychopathology. In *Disori-*
*enting Sexuality: Psychoanalytic Reappraisals of Sexual Identities.* Ed. by T.
Domenici & R. Lesser. New York: Routledge, pp. 33–64.

Domenici, T., & Lesser, R. (Eds.). 1995. *Disorienting Sexuality: Psychoanalytic*
*Reappraisals of Sexual Identities.* New York; Routledge.

Duberman, M., Vicinus, M. & Chauncey, G. Jr., (Eds.). 1989. *Hidden from History:*
*Reclaiming the Gay and Lesbian Past.* New York: New American Library.

Eisenbud, R. 1982. Early and Later Determinants of Lesbian Identity. *Psychoan-*
*alytic Review,* 69(1), 85–109.

Erikson, E. 1985. *The Life Cycle Completed: A Review.* New York: W.W. Norton.

———. 1950. *Childhood and Society.* New York: W.W. Norton [1963].

Faderman, L. 1981. *Surpassing the Love of Men*. New York: Morrow.

———. 1993. Nineteenth-Century Boston Marriage as a Possible Lesson for Today. In *Boston Marriages: Romantic But Asexual Relationships Among Contemporay Lesbians*. Ed. by E. Rothblum & K. Brehony. Amherst: University of Massachusetts Press.

Fairbairn, R. D. 1952. *Psychoanalytic Studies of Personality*. London: Tavistock.

Fast, I. 1984. *Gender Identity*. Hillsdale, NJ: Analytic Press.

Faye, C. 1980. Come Again. In *The Coming Out Stories*. Ed. by J. P. Stanley & S. J. Wolfe. Watertown, MA: Persephone Press, pp. 176–178.

Feinberg, L. 1993. *Stone Butch Blues*. Ithaca, NY: Firebrand Books.

Flaks, D. 1992. Homophobia and the Psychologist's Role in Psychoanalytic Training Institutes. *Psychoanalytic Psychology, 9*, 543–549.

Flax, J. 1993. *Disputed Subjects: Essays on Psychoanalysis, Politics and Philosophy*. New York: Routledge.

———. 1996. Taking Multiplicity Seriously: Some Consequences for Psychoanalytic Theorizing and Practice. *Contemporary Psychoanalysis, 32*(4), 577–594.

Fliegel, Z. 1973. Feminine Psychosexual Development in Freudian Theory. *Psychoanalytic Quarterly, 42*, 385–409.

———. 1982. Current Status of Freud's Controversial Views on Women. *Psychoanalytic Review, 69*, 7–28.

———. 1986. Women's Development in Analytic Theory: Six Decades of Controversy. In *Psychoanalysis and Women: Contemporary Reappraisals*. Ed. by J. Alpert. Hillsdale, NJ: Analytic Press, pp. 3–32.

Foucault, M. 1978. *History of Sexuality: Vol. 1, An Introduction*. Trans. Robert Hurley. New York: Random House.

———. 1979. *Discipline and Punish*. Harmondsworth: Penguin.

———. 1980 *Power/Knowledge: Selected Interviews and Other Writings, 1972–1977*. New York: Pantheon.

Freud, S. 1895. Project for a Scientific Psychology. *Standard Edition, 1*, 295–388. London: Hogarth [1961].

———.1905a. Fragment of an Analysis of a Case of Hysteria. *Standard Edition* 7: 1–122. London: Hogarth [1966].

———. 1905b. Three Essays on the Theory of Sexuality. *Standard Edition, 7*, 125–248. London: Hogarth [1966].

———. 1908. On the Sexual Theories of Children. *Standard Edition, 9*, 209–226. London: Hogarth [1959].

———. 1917. Mourning and Melancholia. *Standard Edition, 14*, 243–258. London: Hogarth [1966].

———. 1920. Psychogenesis of a Case of Female Homosexuality. *Standard Edition, 18*, 145–174. London: Hogarth [1955].

———. 1923. The Ego and the Id. *Standard Edition, 19*, 1–66.. London: Hogarth [1961].

———. 1925. Some Psychical Consequences of the Anatomical Distinction Between the Sexes. *Standard Edition, 19,* 241–258. London: Hogarth [1961].

———. 1931. Female Sexuality. *Standard Edition, 21,* 221–243. London: Hogarth [1966].

———. 1933. Femininity. *Standard Edition, 22,* 112–135. London: Hogarth [1966].

———. 1937. Analysis Terminable and Interminable. *Standard Edition, 23,* 209–245. London: Hogarth [1966].

———. 1940. An Outline of Psychoanalysis. *Standard Edition, 23,* 157–208. London: Hogarth [1966].

Frommer, M. 1994. Homosexuality and Psychoanalysis: Technical Considerations Revisited. *Psychoanalytic Dialogues,* 4(2), 215–232.

Frye, M. 1990. Lesbian "Sex." In *Lesbian Philosophies and Cultures.* Ed. by J. Allen. Albany: State University of New York Press, pp. 305–316.

Garber, E. 1988. Gladys Bentley . . . The Bull Dagger Who Sang the Blues. *OutLook* (Spring), 31.

Garber, M. 1992. *Vested Interests: Cross Dressing & Cultural Anxiety.* New York: Routledge.

———. 1995. *Vice-Versa: Bisexuality and the Eroticism of Everyday Life.* New York: Simon & Schuster.

Ghent, E. 1989. Credo. *Contemporary Psychoanalysis, 25,* 169–211.

Gilligan, C. 1982. Adult Development and Women's Development: Arrangements for a Marriage. In *Women in the Middle Years.* Ed. by J. Giele. New York: Wiley, pp. 89–114.

Glassgold, J. & Iasenza, S. 1995. (Eds.). *Lesbians and Psychoanalysis.* New York: Free Press.

Golden, C. 1987. Diversity and Variability in Women's Sexual Identities. In *Lesbian Psychologies: Explorations and Challenges.* Ed. by the Boston Lesbian Psychologies Collective. Urbana: University of Illinois Press, pp. 18–34.

Goldner, V. 1991. Towards a Critical Relational Theory of Gender. *Psychoanalytic Dialogues,* 1(3), 249–272.

Grahn, J. 1984. *Another Mother Tongue.* Boston: Beacon.

Griggers, C. 1994. The Age of (Post) Mechanical Reproduction. In *The Lesbian Postmodern.* Ed. by L. Doan. New York: Columbia University Press, pp. 118–133.

Grimshaw, J. 1986. *Philosophy and Feminist Thinking.* Minneapolis: University of Minnesota Press.

Grossman, W. 1982. The Self as Fantasy: Fantasy as Theory. *Journal of the American Psychoanalytic Association, 30,* 193–212.

———. 1991. Discussions of "Contemporary Perspectives on Self: Toward an Integration." *Psychoanalytic Dialogues,* 1(2), 149–160.

Grossman,W. & Stewart, W. 1976. Penis Envy: From Childhood to Developmental Metaphor. *Journal of the American Psychoanalytic Association,* *24*(5), 193–212.

Grosz, E. 1994. *Volatile Bodies: Toward a Corporeal Feminism.* Bloomington & Indianapolis: University of Indiana Press.

Hall, M. 1993. "Why Limit Me to Ecstasy?" Towards a Positive Model of Genital Incidentalism Among Friends and Other Lovers. In *Boston Marriages: Romantic but Asexual Relationships Among Contemporay Lesbians.* Ed. by E. Rothblum, & K. Brehony. Amherst: University of Massachusetts Press.

Haraway, D. 1989. A Manifesto for Cyborgs: Science, Technology, and Socialist Feminism in the 1980s. In *Feminism/Postmodernism.* Ed. by L. Nicholson. New York & London: Routledge, pp. 190–233 [1990].

Harris, A. 1991. Gender as Contradiction. *Psychoanalytic Dialogues, 1*(2), 197–224.

———. 1996. The Conceptual Power of Multiplicity. *Contemporary Psychoanalysis, 32*(4), 537–552.

Hoffman, I. 1991. Discussion: Toward a Social-Constructivist View of the Psychoanalytic Situation. *Psychoanalytic Dialogues, 1*(1), 74–105.

Horney, K. 1924. On the Genesis of the Castration Complex in Women. *International Journal of Psychoanalysis 5,* 50–65.

———. 1926. The Flight from Womanhood. *International Journal of Psychoanalysis 7,* 324–339.

———. 1933. The Denial of the Vagina. *International Journal of Psychoanalysis 14,* 57–70.

Ireland, M. 1993. *Reconceiving Women: Separating Motherhood from Female Identity.* New York: Guilford Press.

Irigaray, L. 1985. *Speculum of the Other Woman.* Trans. Gillian C. Gill. Ithaca, NY: Cornell University Press.

———. 1985a. When Our Lips Speak Together. In *The Sex Which Is Not One.* Ithaca, NY: Cornell University Press.

———. 1991. The Limits of Transference. In *The Irigaray Reader* Ed. by M. Whitford. Oxford: Basil Blackwell.

Isay, R. 1989. *Being Homosexual, Gay Men and Their Development.* New York: Farrar, Straus & Giroux.

Jones, E. 1927. The Early Development of Female Sexuality. *International Journal of Psychoanalysis, 8*(4), 457–472.

Kane, E. 1988. *Birth Mother: America's First Legal Surrogate Mother, Her Change of Heart.* New York: Harcourt Brace.

Kanefield, L. 1985. Psychoanalytic Constructions of Female Development and Women's Conflicts About Achievement. *Journal of the American Academy of Psychoanalysis, 13,* 229–247.

Kanter, R. 1977. *Men and Women of the Corporation.* New York: Basic Books.

Kaplan, L. 1978. *Oneness and Separateness*. New York: Simon & Schuster.

Katz, J. (Ed.) 1976. *Gay American History: Lesbian and Gay Men in the U.S.A.* New York: Thomas Crowell.

Kirkpatrick, M., Smith, C. & Roy R., 1981. Lesbian Mothers and Their Children: A Comparative Survey. *American Journal of Orthopsychiatry, 51*, 541–555.

Kleeman, J. 1976. Freud's Views on Early Female Sexuality in the Light of Direct Child Observation. *Journal of the the American Psychoanalytic Association*, 24(5), 3–28.

Klein, M. 1928. Early Stages of the Oedipus Complex. *International Journal of Psychoanalysis. 9*, 167–180.

——. 1952. The Origins of Transference. In *The Selected Papers of Melanie Klein*. Ed. by J. Mitchell. New York: Free Press, pp. 201–210 [1986].

Kohlberg, L. 1966. A Cognitive–Developmental Analysis of Children's Sexual Concepts and Attitudes. In *The Development of Sex Differences*. Ed. by E. Maccoby. Palo Alto, CA: Stanford University Press.

Kohut, H. 1982. Introspection, Empathy and the Semi–Circle of Mental Health. *International Journal of Psychoanalysis, 63*, 395–407.

Kotre, J. 1984. *Outliving the Self: Generativity and the Interpretation of Lives*. Balitmore: Johns Hopkins University Press.

Kuhn, T. 1962. *The Structure of Scientific Revolutions*. Chicago: University of Chicago Press.

Kulish, N. 1986. Gender and Transference: the Screen of the Phallic Mother. *International Revue of Psychoanalysis, 3*, 393–404.

——. 1991. Representations of the Clitoris. *Psychoanalytic Inquiry, 11*(4), 511–536.

Kwawer, J. 1980. Transference and Countertransference in Homosexuality— Changes in Psychoanalytic Views. *American Journal of Psychotherapy, 34*(1), 72–80.

Lacan, J. 1960. The Subversion of the Subject and the Dialectic of Desire in the Freudian Unconscious. *In Ecrits: A Selection*. London: Tavistock. pp. 292–235 [1977].

——. 1977. *Ecrits*. London: Tavistock.

Levenson, E. 1974. Changing concepts of intimacy in psychoanalytic practice. *Contemporary Psychoanalysis, 10*(3), 359–371.

Levenson, E. 1991. *The Purloined Self*. New York: Contemporary Psychoanalysis Books.

Levinson, D. 1978. *The Season's Of a Man's Life*. New York: Knopf.

Levy–Warren, M. 1996. *The Adolescent Journey*. Northvale, NJ: Jason Aronson.

Lewes, K. 1988. *The Psychoanalytic Theory of Male Homosexuality*. New York: Simon & Schuster.

Lewin, E. 1993. *Lesbian Mothers: Accounts of Gender in American Culture*. Ithaca, NY: Cornell University Press.

Lewin, E. & Lyons, T. 1982. Everything in Its Place: The Coexistence of Lesbianism and Motherhood. In *Homosexuality: Social, Psychological and Biological Issues*. Ed. by P. Weinrich, J. Gonsiorek, & M. Hotvedt. Beverly Hills, CA: Sage, pp. 249–274.

Lichtenberg, J. 1981. Implications for Psychoanalytic Theory of Research on the Neonate. *International Review of Psychoanalysis, 8*, 35–53.

———. 1983. *Psychoanalysis and Infant Research*. Hillsdale, NJ: Analytic Press.

Linden, R., Pagano, D., Russell, D., & Star, S. 1982. *Against Sadomasochism: A Radical Feminist Analysis*. East Palo Alto, CA: Frog in the Wall.

Lindenbaum, J. 1985. The Shattering of Illusions: The Problem of Competition in Lesbian Relationships. *Feminist Studies, 11*(1) (Spring).

Loewald, H. 1973. On Internalization. *Papers on Psychoanalysis*. New Haven & London: Yale University Press, pp.69–86 [1980].

Lorde, A. 1982. Zami: A New Spelling of My Name. In *Zami, Sister, Outsider*. New York: Quality Paperback Book Club [1993].

Lyotard, J. 1984. *The Postmodern Condition: A Report on Knowledge*. Manchester, UK: University of Manchester Press.

Magee, M., & Miller, D. 1992. She Foreswore Her Womanhood: Psychoanalytic Views of Female Homosexuality. *Clinical Social Work Journal, 20*(1), 67–87.

Mahler, M., Pine, F., & Bergman, A. 1975. *On Human Symbiosis and the Viscissitudes of Human Individuation*. New York: International Universities Press.

Mahoney, M., & Yugvesson, B. 1992. The Construction of Subjectivity and the Paradox of Resistance. *Signs* (Autumn), 44–73.

Main, M., Kaplan, N., & Cassidy, J. 1985. Security in Infancy, Childhood and Adulthood: A Move to the Level of Representation. In *Growing Points in Attachment Theory and Research. Monographs of the Society for Research in Child Development, 50*(1–2, Serial No. 209): 66–104. Ed. by I. Bretherton & E. Waters.

Margolies, L., Becker M., & Jackson–Brewer K. 1987. Internalized Homophobia: Identifying and Treating the Oppressor Within. In *Lesbian Psychologies: Explorations and Challenges*. Ed. by the Boston Lesbian Psychologies Collective. Urbana: University of Illinois Press, pp. 220–241.

McAdams, D. 1985. *Power, Intimacy and the Life Story: Personalogical Inquiries into Identity*. New York: Guilford.

McAdams, D., Ruetzel, K., & Foley, J. 1986. Complexity and Generativity at Mid–Life: Relations Among Social Motives, Ego Development, and Adults' Plans for the Future. *Journal of Personality and Social Psychology, 50*(4), 800–807.

McAdams, D., & St. Aubin, E. 1992. A Theory of Generativity and Its Assessment Through Self–Report, Behavioral Acts and Narrative Themes in Autobiography. *Journal of Personality and Social Psychology, 62*(6), 1003–1015.

McCandlish, B. 1987. Against All Odds: Lesbian Mother Family Dynamics. In *Gay and Lesbian Parents*. Ed. by F. Bozett. New York: Praeger. pp. 23–36.

McDougall, J. 1980. *Plea for a Measure of Abnormality*. New York: International Universities Press.

———. 1986. Eve's Reflection: On the Homosexual Components of Female Sexuality. *In Between Analyst and Patient: Dimensions in Countertransference and Transference*. Ed. by H. Meyers. Hillsdale, NJ: Analytic Press.

———. 1991. Sexual Identity, Trauma and Creativity. *Psychoanalytic Inquiry*, *11*(4), 559–581.

*M Butterfly* written by David Henry Hwang Director David Cronenburg

Mitchell, S. 1981. The Psychoanalytic Treatment of Homosexuality: Some Technical Considerations. *International Revue of Psychoanalysis, 8,* 63–80.

———. 1988. *Relational Concepts in Psychoanalysis*. Cambridge: Harvard University Press.

———. 1991. Contemporary Perspectives on Self: Toward an Integration. *Psychoanalytic Dialogues, 1*(2), 121–147.

———. 1992. True Selves, False Selves, and the Ambiguity of Authenticity. In *Relational Perspectives in Psychoanalysis*. Ed. by N. Skolnick & S. Warshaw. Hillsdale, NJ: The Analytic Press.

———. 1993. *Hope and Dread in Psychoanalysis*. New York: Basic Books.

Moi, T. 1981. Representations of Patriarchy: Sexuality and Epistemology in Freud's Dora. *Feminist Review* (October), 60–73.

Moulton, R. 1986. Professional Success, A Conflict for Women. In *Psychoanalysis and Women: Contemporary Reappraisals*. Ed. by J. Alpert. Hillsdale, NJ: Analytic Press, pp. 161–181.

Newman, L. 1989. *Heather Has Two Mommies*. Illustrated by Diana Souza. Northampton, MA: In Other Words Press.

Nichols, M. 1987. Doing Sex Therapy with Lesbians: Bending a Heterosexual Paradigm to Fit a Gay Life–Style. In *Lesbian Psychologies: Explorations and Challenges*. Ed. by the Boston Lesbian Psychologies Collective. Urbana: University of Illinois Press, pp. 242–260.

Nicolosi, J. 1991. *Reparative Therapy of Male Homosexuality*. Northvale, NJ: Jason Aronson.

O'Connor, N. 1995. Passionate Differences: Lesbianism, Post–Modernism, and Psychoanalysis. In *Disorienting Sexuality: Psychoanalytic Reappraisals of Sexual Identities*. Ed. by T. Domenici & R. Lesser. New York: Routledge, pp. 167–176.

O'Connor, N, & Ryan, J. 1993. *Wild Desires and Mistaken Identities*. New York: Columbia University Press.

Ogden, T. 1989. *The Primitive Edge of Experience*. Northvale, NJ: Jason Aronson.

Patterson, C. 1992. Children of Lesbian and Gay Parents. *Child Development, 63,* 1025–1042.

Person, E. 1982. Women Working: Fears of Failure, Deviance and Success. *Journal of the American Academy of Psychoanalysis, 10*, 67–84.

Phillips, A. 1995. Keep it Moving—Commentary on Judith Butler's "Melancholic Gender–Refused Identifications." *Psychoanalytic Dialogues, 5*(2), 181–188.

Racker, H. 1968. *Transference and Countertransference*. New York: International University Press.

Radicalesbians. 1973, Woman-Identified Woman. In *Radical Feminism*. Ed. by A. Koedt, E. Levine, & A. Rapone. New York: Quadrangle. First published in *Notes from the Third Year* [1971]. As quoted in Bat–Ami Bar On, The Feminist Sexuality Debates and the Transformation of the Political, *Hypatia, 7*(4), 48, (1992).

Ramos, M. 1980. Freud's Dora, Dora's Hysteria: The Negation of Woman's Rebellion. *Feminist Studies, 6*, 472–510.

Rich, A. 1972. The Stranger. *Diving into the Wreck*. New York: W. W. Norton, p. 19.

———. 1981. Compulsory Heterosexuality and Lesbian Existence. In *The Lesbian and Gay Studies Reader*. Ed. by H. Abelove, M. Barale, & D. Halperin. New York: Routledge [1993], pp. 227–254.

Riviere, J. 1929. Womanliness as a Masquerade. *International Journal of Psychoanalysis, 9*, 303–313.

Roof, J. 1991. *A Lure of Knowledge: Lesbian Sexuality and Theory*. New York: Columbia University Press.

Rose, J. 1978, Dora—Fragment of an Analysis. *m/f, 2*, 5–21.

———. 1986. *Sexuality in the Field of Vision*. London: Verso.

Roth, S. 1988. A Woman's Homosexual Transference with a Male Analyst. *Psychoanalytic Quarterly, 57*, 28–55.

Rothblum, E. 1994. Transforming Lesbian Sexuality. *Psychology of Women Quarterly, 18*(4), 627–641.

Rothblum, E. & Brehony, K. (Eds.). 1993. *Boston Marriages: Romantic but Asexual Relationships Among Contemporay Lesbians*. Amherst: University of Massachusetts Press.

Rothman, B. 1988. Reproductive Technology and the Commodification of Life. In *Embryos, Ethics and Women's Rights*. Ed. by D. Baruch, A. Adorno Jr., & J. Seager. New York: Harrington Park Press.

———. 1989a. On Surrogacy: Constructing Social Policy. In *Gender in Transition: A New Frontier*. Ed. by J. Offerman-Zuckerberg, New York: Plenum, pp. 227–233.

———. 1989b. *Recreating Motherhood: Ideology and Technology in a Patriarchal Society*. New York: Norton.

Rubin, G. 1984. Thinking Sex: Notes for a Radical Theory of the Politics of Sexuality. In *Pleasure and Danger: Exploring Female Sexuality*. Ed. by C. Vance. New York: Routledge & Kegan Paul. Also in *The Lesbian and Gay Studies Reader*. Ed. by H. Abelove, M. Barale, & D. Halperin. New York: Routledge, pp. 1–44 (1993).

———. 1992. Of Catmites and Kings: Reflections on Butch, Gender and Boundaries. In *The Persistent Desire: A Femme-Butch Reader*. Ed. by J. Nestle. Boston: Alyson, pp. 466–482.

Rubin, G., with Butler, J. 1994. Sexual traffic. *Differences*, 6 (2&3), 62–99.

Rubin, J., Provenzano, F., & Luria, Z. 1974. The Eye of the Beholder: Parents' Views on Sex of Newborns. *American Journal of Orthopsychiatry*, 44, 512–519.

Ruddick, S. 1989. *Maternal Thinking*. Boston: Beacon.

Ryff, C., & Heincke, S. 1983. Subjective Organization of Personality in Adulthood and Aging. *Journal of Personality and Social Psychology*, 44, 807–816.

Sackville-West, V. 1991. *Saint Joan of Arc*. New York: Doubleday.

Samois. 1981. *Coming to Power*. Palo Alto, CA: Up Press.

Schoenberg, E. 1995. Psychoanalytic Theories of Lesbian Desire. In *Disorienting Sexuality: Psychoanalytic Reappraisals of Sexual Identities*. Ed. by T. Domenici & R. Lesser. New York: Routledge, pp. 203–226.

Schwartz, A. 1984a. Psychoanalysis and Women: A Rapprochement. *Women & Therapy*, 3(1): 3–12.

———. 1984b. On Choosing To Be a Lesbian: Conflicts in Gender Role Identity and Their Clinical Implications. Presented at the Annual Meeting of the Association for Women in Psychology, Boston, MA.

———. 1986. Some Notes on the Development of Female Gender Role Identity. *Psychoanalysis and Women: Contemporary Reappraisals*. Ed. by J. Alpert. Hillsdale,NJ: Analytic Press. pp. 57–79.

———. 1988a. Lesbians in Treatment. Presented at the Harvard Medical School Department of Continuing Education, Boston, MA.

———. 1988b. Lesbian Parenting: Issues of Generativity and Gender Role Identity. Presented at the Psychoanalytic Society's Fourth Biennial Conference: Unique Family Configurations, Neglected Family Ties: Psychoanalytic Perspectives, New York University.

———. 1989. Earliest Memories: Sex Differences and the Meaning of Experience. In *Representation: Social Constructions of Gender*. Ed. by R. Unger. New York: Baywood, pp. 236–244. Also in *Imagination, Cognition and Personality*, 4(1).

———. 1993. Thoughts on the Construction of Maternal Representations. *Psychoanalytic Psychology*, 10(3), 331–344.

———. 1994. Gender and Generativity. *Psychoanalysis and Psychotherapy*, 11(1), 25–33.

———. 1996. *Coming Out/Being Heard*. Presented at the Annual Spring Meeting of the American Psychological Association, Division of Psychoanalysis in New York City.

———. In press. Postmodern Masquerade: Re-Visiting Riviere. Commentary on Joan Riviere's "Womanliness as a Masquerade." In *Women in Psychoanalysis: A Continuing Dailogue*, Ed. by D. Bassin, Northvale, NJ: Jason Aronson.

Schwartz, D. 1993. Heterophilia—The Love That Dare Not Speak Its Aim. *Psychoanalytic Dialogues, 3*(4), 643–652.

———. 1995a. Current Psychoanalytic Discourses on Sexuality. In *Disorienting Sexuality: Psychoanalytic Reappraisals of Sexual Identities.* Ed. by T. Domenici & R. Lesser. New York: Routledge, pp. 115–128.

———. 1995b. Retaining Classical Concepts-Hidden Costs: Commentary on Lewis Aron's "The Internalized Primal Scene." *Psychoanalytic Dialogues, 5*(2), 239–248.

Seligman, S. & Shanok, R. 1995. Subjectivity, Complexity, and the Social World: Erikson's Identity Concept and Contemporary Relational Theories. *Psychoanalytic Dialogues, 5*(4), 537–566.

Sherif, C. 1982. Needed Concepts in the Study of Gender Identity. *Psychology of Women Quarterly, 6,* 375–398.

Siegel, E. 1988. *Female Homosexuality: Choice Without Volition.* Hillsdale, NJ: Analytic Press.

Silverman, D. 1986. Some Proposed Modifications of Psychoanalytic Theories of Early Childhood Development. In *Empirical Studies of Psychoanalytic Theories,* Vol. 2. Ed. by J. Masling. Hillside, NJ: Analytic Press.

———. 1993. Attachment Research: An Approach to a Developmental Relational Perspective. In *Relational Perspectives in Psychoanalysis.* Ed. by N. Skolnick & S. Warshaw. Hillsdale, NJ: Analytic Press, pp. 195–216.

Singer, B., & Descamps, D. (Eds.). 1994. *Gay and Lesbian Stats.* New York: New Press.

Smith-Rosenberg, C. 1985. *Disorderly Conduct.* Oxford: Oxford University Press.

Snitow, A. 1989. A Gender Diary. In *Rocking the Ship of State: Feminist Peace Politics.* Ed. by A. Harris & Y. King. Denver: Westview.

Socarides,C. 1978. *Homosexuality.* New York: Aronson.

Spence, D. 1982. *Narrative Truth and Historical Truth.* New York: W.W. Norton.

Spieler, S. 1986. The Gendered Self. In *Psychoanalysis and Women: Contemporary Reappraisals.* Ed. by J. Alpert. Hillsdale, NJ: Analytic Press, pp. 33–56.

Stern, D. 1985. *The Interpersonal World of the Infant.* New York: Basic Books.

———. 1989. The Representation of Relational Patterns: Developmental Considerations. In *Relationship Disturbances in Early Childhood.* Ed. by A. Sameroff & R. Emde. New York: Basic Books.

Stoller, R. 1968. *Sex and Gender: The Development of Masculinity and Femininity.* New York: Science House.

———. 1973. *Splitting: A Case of Female Masculinity.* New York: Quadrangle/New York Times Book Co.

Storey, J. 1993. *Cultural Theory and Popular Culture.* Athens: University of Georgia Press.

Suleiman, S. 1986. (Re)Writing the Body: The Politics and Poetics of Female Eroticism. In *The Female Body in Western Culture.* Ed. by S. Suleiman. Cambridge: Harvard University Press, pp. 7–29.

Taylor, K. 1971. *Generations of Denial: 75 Short Biographies of Women's History*. New York: Times Change Press.

Turque, B. 1992. Gays Under Fire. *Newsweek*, September 4.

Tyson, P. 1982. A Developmental Line of Gender Identity, Gender Role and Choice of Love Object. *Journal of the American Psychoanalytic Association, 30*(1), 29–60.

Vicinus, M. 1993. They Wonder to Which Sex I Belong. In *The Lesbian and Gay Studies Reader*. Ed. by H. Abelove, M. Barale, & D. Halperin. New York: Routledge, pp. 432–452.

Weston, K. 1991. *Families We Choose: Lesbians, Gays, Kinship*. New York: Columbia University Press.

Wickes, G. 1977. *The Amazon Letters: The Life and Loves of Natalie Barney*. London: W. H. Allen

Winnicott, D. W. 1956. Primary Maternal Pre-occupation. In *Collected Papers: Through Paediatrics to Psychoanalysis*. New York: Basic Books, pp.300–305 [1958].

———. 1960. Ego Distortion in Terms of True and False Self. In *The Maturational Processes and the Facilitating Environment*. New York: International Universities Press, pp. 140–152 [1965].

———. 1963. The Development of the Capacity for Concern. In *The Maturational Processes and the Facilitating Environment*. New York: International Universitities Press pp. 73–83 [1965].

———. 1971. *Playing and Reality*. New York: Basic Books.

Wittig, M. 1975. *The Lesbian Body*. Trans. David LeVay. Boston: Beacon.

———. 1980. The Straight Mind, *Feminist Issues, 1*(1), 103–111.

———. 1981. One is Not Born a Woman. *Feminist Issues, 2*(1): 47–54.

———. 1982. The Category of Sex. In *The Straight Mind. . . and Other Essays*. Boston: Beacon, pp. 1–8 [1992].

———. 1992. *The Straight Mind. . . and Other Essays*. Boston: Beacon.

Wrye, H. & Welles, J. 1994. *The Narration of Desire: Erotic Transferences and Countertransferences*. Hillsdale, NJ: Analytic Press.

Zita, J. 1992. The Male Lesbian and the Postmodernist Body. *Hypatia, 7*(4), 106–127.

# index